CONTINENTAL AFRICA

CONTINENTAL EUROPE 60

A DORLING KINDERSLEY BOOK

PROJECT CARTOGRAPHY AND DESIGN
Julia Lunn   Peter Winfield

CARTOGRAPHIC RESEARCH
Michael Martin

PROJECT EDITOR AND INDEX-GAZETTEER
Jayne Parsons

DIGITAL BASE MAPS PRODUCED ON DK CARTOPIA BY
Simon Lewis   Rob Stokes   Thomas Robertshaw

PRODUCTION CONTROLLER
Hilary Stephens

EDITORIAL DIRECTOR
Andrew Heritage

ART DIRECTOR
Chez Picthall

First published in Great Britain in 1996
by Dorling Kindersley Limited
9 Henrietta Street, London WC2E 8PS

Copyright © 1996 Dorling Kindersley Limited, London

A CIP catalogue record for this book is available from the British Library

ISBN: 0-7513-0241-4

*Film output in England by Euroscan
Printed and bound in Italy by L.E.G.O*

DORLING KINDERSLEY
ULTIMATE POCKET

WORLD
ATLAS

LONDON • NEW YORK • STUTTGART • MOSCOW

KEY

——	*International border*
– –	*Disputed border*
– · –	*Claimed border*
~	*International border along river*
——	*State border*
~	*State border along river*
~	*River*
⌣	*Lake*
~	*Canal*
~	*Seasonal river*
⌣	*Seasonal lake*
⤙	*Waterfall*
——	*Road*
——	*Railway*
●	*Capital city*
◎	*Major town*
○	*Minor town*
●	*Major port*
·	*Minor port*
✈	*International airport*
▲	*Spot height – metres*
·	*Spot depth – metres*

CONTENTS

THE PHYSICAL WORLD

THE POLITICAL WORLD

8   *For full list of abbreviations see page 134.*

TIME ZONES

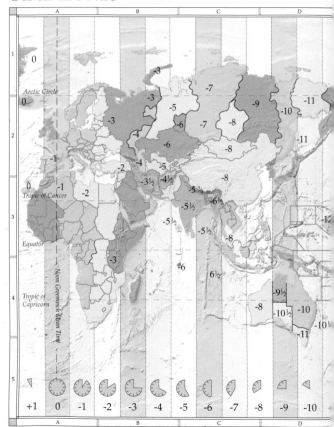

Numbers on the map indicate the number of hours which must be added or subtracted, as appropriate, in that time zone to reach GMT.

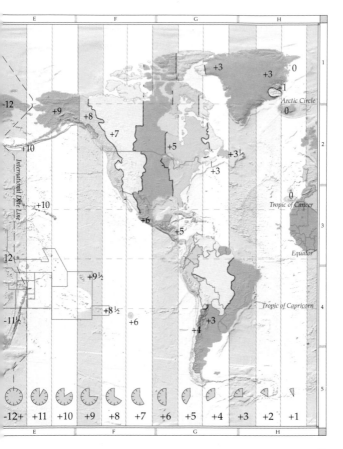

THE ARCTIC OCEAN

ASIA

Tiksi · Leud

Laptev Sea

New Siberian Is.
(Russ. Fed.)

Severnaya Zemlya
(Russ. Fed.)

East Siberian Sea

Pevek ·

Wrangel I.
(Russ. Fed.)

Arctic Circle

Chukchi Sea

Bering Strait

Limit of permanent pack ice

ARCTIC OCEAN

Lomonosov (Harris) Ridge

Fram (Angara) Basin

Canada
(Laurentian)
Basin

NORTH AMERICA

Beaufort Sea

Mackenzie

Tuktoyaktuk ·

Banks I.
(Canada)

Melville I.
(Canada)

Prince Patrick I.
(Canada)

Bathurst I.
(Canada)

Queen Elizabeth Is.
(Canada)

Axel Heiberg I.
(Canada)

0 km   500

0 miles   500

CONTINENTAL NORTH AMERICA

ARCTIC OCEAN

12

Chukchi
Sea

Limit of permanent pack-ice

Beaufort
Sea
2761m

Brooks Range

Melville I.
Viscount Melville Sound
Banks I.

Amundsen Gulf
Victoria I.

92

Arctic Circle

ASIA

Bering Strait

USA
(Alaska)
Denali
6194m

Mackenzie

Great
Bear Lake

St Lawrence I.

Alaska Range

Mt. Logan
6050m

Great
Slave Lake

Nunivak I.

Alaska
Peninsula

Kodiak I.

Bering
Sea

Aleutian Islands

Aleutian Trench

Queen
Charlotte Is.

Queen Charlotte
Sound

Gulf
of
Alaska

Vancouver I.
Mt. Rainier
4392m
Mt. St Helens
2550m

Rocky Mountains

Great

C A N

U

Blac
Hill

122

PACIFIC

OCEAN

Cascade Range

Great
Basin

Great
Salt Lake

Death
Valley

Mt. Whitney
4417m

Colorado
Plateau

Sonoran
Desert

Sierra Ma

Gulf of California

Tropic of Cancer

USA
(Hawaiian Is.)

Baja
California

Colin
4330

0 km   1000

0 miles   1000

Axel Heiberg I.
Ellesmere I.
Queen Elizabeth Is.
Devon I.
Knud Rasmussen Land
Lancaster Sound
Prince of Wales I.
Somerset I.
Baffin I.
Baffin Bay
Greenland (Denmark)
Gunnbjørn Field ▲ 3700m
Arctic Circle
Southampton I.
Hudson Strait
Iceland
Reindeer Lake
Hudson Bay
Ungava Peninsula
Ungava Bay
Labrador
Labrador Sea
EUROPE
60 ▷
Belcher Is.
L. Winnipeg
James Bay
Labrador Basin
A
D
A
Laurentian Plateau
Strait of Belle Isle
Missouri
L. Superior
Great Lakes
St. Lawrence
Newfoundland
Gulf of St. Lawrence
St Pierre & Miquelon (France)
C. Race
Grand Banks
Platte
L. Huron
L. Michigan
L. Ontario
L. Erie
Niagara Falls
Ohio
Cape Cod
Arkansas
Red R.
2037m ▲ Appalachian Mts.
Sohm Plain
Cape Hatteras
Bermuda (UK)
Azores (Portugal)
46 ▷
P l a i n s
A T L A N T I C
Mississippi
Mississippi Delta
The Everglades
Nares Plain
O C E A N
Citlaltépetl 5700m ▲
Gulf of Mexico
MEXICO
Straits of Florida
BAHAMAS
CUBA
Turks & Caicos Is. (UK)
DOMINICAN REP.
Puerto Rico (USA)
British Virgin Is. (UK)
Anguilla (UK)
Tropic of Cancer
▲ 5747m
Cayman Is. (UK)
JAMAICA
HAITI
(USA) Virgin Is.
ANTIGUA & BARBUDA
Montserrat (UK)
48 ▷
BELIZE
GUATEMALA
HONDURAS
ST KITTS & NEVIS
ST LUCIA
Guadeloupe (France)
DOMINICA
Martinique (France)
EL SALVADOR
NICARAGUA
Caribbean Sea
Aruba (Neth.)
Neth. Antilles
BARBADOS
GRENADA
ST VINCENT & THE GRENADINES
COSTA RICA
PANAMA
TRINIDAD & TOBAGO
36 ▷
SOUTH AMERICA

E   F   G   H

WESTERN CANADA & ALASKA

RUSSIAN
FEDERATION

Wrangel I.

ARCT

OCE

Arctic Circle

Bering Strait

Attu I.

*Bering
Sea*

Prudho
Bay

Kiska I.

St. Lawrence I.

Brooks Range

ALASKA
(USA)

Nunivak I.

Yukon

Fairbanks

Aleutian Islands

Alaska Range

Dawso

Umnak I.
Dutch Harbor
Unalaska I.

Anchorage

Valdez

YUKON
TERRITOR

Aleutian Trench

Kodiak I. Kodiak

Cordova

WHITEHORSE

*Gulf
of
Alaska*

JUNEAU

PACIFIC

OCEAN

Ketchikan

Prince Rupert

Queen Charlotte Is.

*Queen Charlotte
Sound*

Port Alice

Vancouver I.

VICTOR

16

0 km   400

0 miles   400

EASTERN CANADA

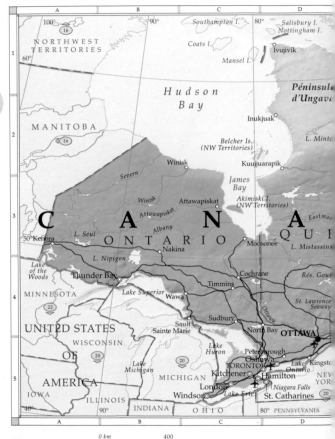

0 km   400

0 miles   400

Baffin I.
70°   60°   50°   60°

Labrador Sea

Labrador Basin

dson Strait
Akpatok I.
(NW Territories)
C. Chidley

Ungava Bay

Kuujjuaq

ATLANTIC OCEAN

oNain

Hopedale
Makkovik

Scefferville

Labrador

Cartwright

NEWFOUNDLAND

Port Hope Simpson

Réservoir
aniapiscau

Smallwood
Reservoir

Churchill Falls

Happy Valley-
Goose Bay

Strait of Belle Isle

Labrador City

50°

Newfoundland

D   **E**   **C**   **A**

Réservoir
Manicouagan

Havre-
Saint-Pierre

Gander

Grand Falls

Clarenville

ST JOHN'S

Sept-Îles

Île d'Anticosti

Corner Brook

Saint-Jean
Jonquière

Gaspé

Gulf of St.Lawrence

St. Lawrence

Channel-Port-aux-Basques

C. Race

St Pierre

Chicoutimi

Bathurst

PRINCE
EDWARD
ISLAND

Cabot Strait

St Pierre & Miquelon
(France)

Grand Banks

QUÉBEC

NEW
BRUNSWICK

FREDERICTON

Sydney

Trois-Rivières

MAINE

Moncton

CHARLOTTETOWN

Sherbrooke

20

Saint John

NOVA SCOTIA

ntreal

Dartmouth
HALIFAX

Sohm Plain

NEW
HAMPSHIRE

Yarmouth

C. Sable

VERMONT

MASSACHUSETS

ATLANTIC OCEAN

RHODE ISLAND

70°

60°

CONNECTICUT

USA: THE NORTHEAST

0 km   200

0 miles   200

USA: Central States

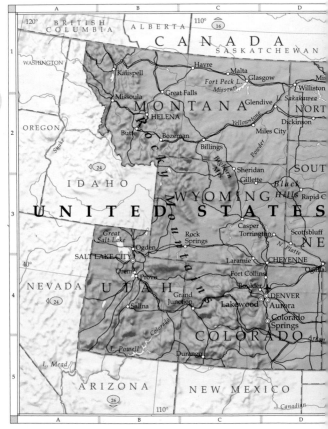

USA: The West

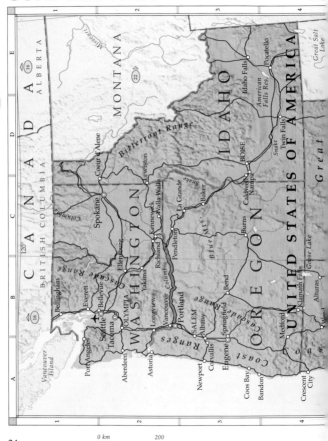

0 km   200

0 miles   200

USA: THE SOUTHWEST

0 km   200

0 miles   200

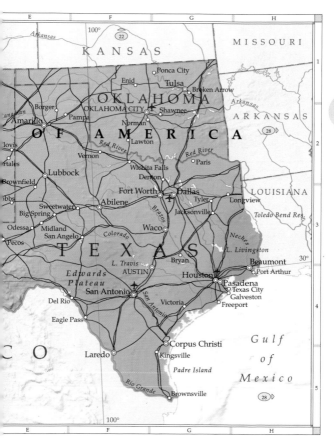

USA: The Southeast

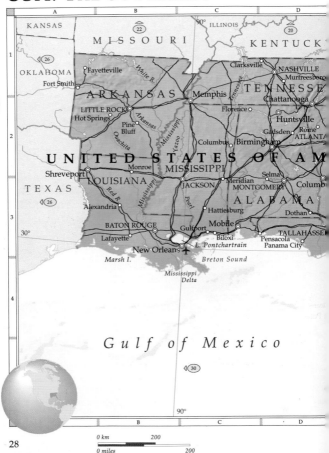

0 km 200

0 miles 200

MEXICO

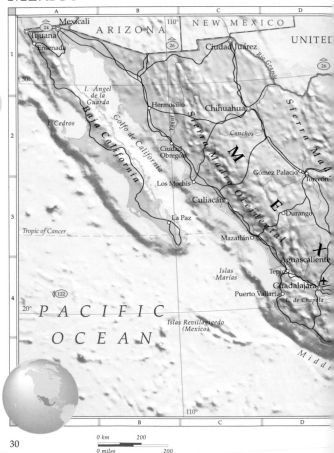

0 km · · · · 200
0 miles · · · · 200

Cayman Trench

Islas Santanilla
(Honduras)

JAMAICA

Greater Antilles

HAITI

Bajo Nuevo
(Colombia)

(34)

C a r i b b e a n

S e a

Cayos Miskitos
(Nicaragua)

I. de Providencia
(Colombia)

I. de San Andrés
(Colombia)

Islas del Maiz (Nicaragua)

uefields

COSTA
RICA

Limón

artago

PANAMA

Colón

PANAMA CITY

Gulf
of
Darien

Penonomé
Panama
Canal

Isla del
Rey

David

Santiago

Chitré

Golfo
de
Panamá

COLOMBIA

Golfo
de
Chiriquí

Las Tablas

(38)

THE CARIBBEAN

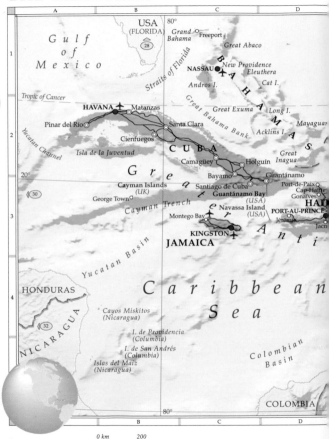

USA
(FLORIDA)
80°

Gulf of Mexico

Grand Bahama
Freeport
Great Abaco

NASSAU
New Providence
Eleuthera

Andros I.
Cat I.

Straits of Florida

Tropic of Cancer

HAVANA
Matanzas

Pinar del Rio

Santa Clara

Yucatan Channel

Cienfuegos

Isla de la Juventud

CUBA

Great Bahama Bank

Great Exuma
Long I.

Acklins I.
Mayaguar

Great Inagua

Camagüey
Holguín

Greater

20°

Bayamo
Guantánamo

Santiago de Cuba

Cayman Islands
(UK)

George Town

Cayman Trench

Guantánamo Bay
(USA)

Navassa Island
(USA)

Montego Bay

KINGSTON

JAMAICA

Port-de-Paix
Cap-Haïtie
Gonaïves

PORT-AU-PRINCE

Jérémie

HAIT

Jacm

Antil

Yucatan Basin

HONDURAS

Cayos Miskitos
(Nicaragua)

I. de Providencia
(Columbia)

I. de San Andrés
(Columbia)

Islas del Maíz
(Nicaragua)

NICARAGUA

Caribbean Sea

Colombian Basin

80°

COLOMBIA

0 km   200

0 miles   200

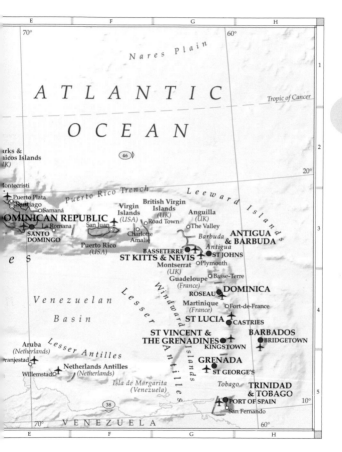

70°   60°

Nares Plain

ATLANTIC

OCEAN

Tropic of Cancer

rks &
icos Islands
(K)

20°

ontecristi

Puerto Rico Trench   *Leeward Islands*

Puerto Plata
Santiago
Samaná
DOMINICAN REPUBLIC
La Romana   San Juan
SANTO
DOMINGO
Virgin   British Virgin
Islands   Islands
(USA)   (UK)
Road Town
Charlotte
Amalie
Puerto Rico
(USA)

Anguilla
(UK)
The Valley

Barbuda

ANTIGUA
& BARBUDA

BASSETERRE   Antigua   ST JOHNS
ST KITTS & NEVIS   Plymouth
Montserrat
(UK)
Guadeloupe   Basse-Terre
(France)
ROSEAU   DOMINICA
Martinique   Fort-de-France
(France)
ST LUCIA   CASTRIES

e s

Venezuelan

Basin

Aruba
(Netherlands)
ranjestad
Willemstad

Lesser Antilles

Netherlands Antilles
(Netherlands)

Isla de Margarita
(Venezuela)

ST VINCENT &
THE GRENADINES   KINGSTOWN

BARBADOS
BRIDGETOWN

GRENADA
ST GEORGE'S

Tobago   TRINIDAD
& TOBAGO
PORT OF SPAIN
San Fernando

Lesser Antilles   *Windward Islands*

10°

70°   VENEZUELA   60°

E   F   G   H

CONTINENTAL SOUTH AMERICA

ATLANTIC OCEAN

Mid-Atlantic Ridge

Tropic of Capricorn

Equator

Ilha Fernando de Noronha (Brazil)

Cabo de São Roque

Represa de Sobradinho

Amazon Delta

Ilha de Marajó

2787m Mar

Tocantins

B r a z i l i a n   Highlands

2033m

São Francisco

Lesser Antilles

Trinidad

French Guiana (France)

SURINAM

GUYANA

VENEZUELA

Angel Falls 980m

Guiana Highlands

3014m

Rio Negro

A m a z o n i a

Japurá

Xingu

Tapajós

Madeira

B R A Z I L

Aquarico

Planalto do Mato Grosso

Pantanal

Paraguay

G r a n   C h a c o

PARAG

BOLIVIA

Netherlands Antilles

Caribbean Sea

Gulf of Darien

COLOMBIA

Caquetá

Cotopaxi 5896m

Chimborazo 6267m

Marañón

ECUADOR

Apure

Orinoco

Rio Branco

Purus

Juruá

P E R U

A N D E S

Salar de Uyuni

Guallatiri 6060m

Peru-Chile Trench

CENTRAL AMERICA

Middle America Trench

Gulf of Guayaquil

Galápagos Is. (Ecuador)

Huascarán 6768m

Equator

PACIFIC OCEAN

5800m

46

14

122

0 km   1000

0 miles   1000

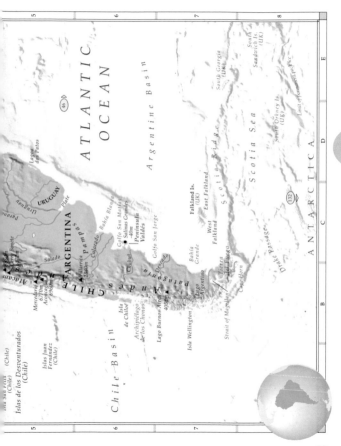

ATLANTIC
OCEAN

Argentine Basin

Chile Basin

URUGUAY

Plate

ARGENTINA

CHILE

Andes

Patagonia

Islas Juan
Fernández
(Chile)

Islas de los Desventurados
(Chile)

Isla San Félix (Chile)

Laguna
de los Patos

Salado

Colorado
Bahía Blanca

Golfo San Matías
Salinas Grandes
-40m
Península
Valdés

Golfo San Jorge

Bahía
Grande

Lago
Argentino

Deseado

Chubut

Lago Buenos Aires

Isla Wellington

Isla
de Chiloé

Archipiélago
de los Chonos

Aconcagua
6960m
Mercedario
6770m

Tupungato
Maipo
Ojos del Salado
Llullaillaco

Atacama

Tierra
del Fuego

Cape Horn

Strait of Magellan

Drake Passage

Scotia Sea

Scotia Ridge

Falkland Is.
(UK)
East Falkland
West
Falkland

South Georgia
(UK)

South
Sandwich Is.
(UK)

South Orkney Is.
(UK)

Limit of Continental Ice Sheet

ANTARCTICA

37

NORTHERN SOUTH AMERICA

0 km 200
0 miles 200

Antilles GRENADA 60°

ATLANTIC

OCEAN

Isla de Margarita
Carúpano
TRINIDAD
& TOBAGO

aiquetia
Cumaná

Barcelona

Maturín

El Tigre

Tucupita

Ciudad Bolívar
Ciudad Guayana

Morawhanna

ZUELA

Cuyuni

GEORGETOWN
New Amsterdam

Bartica

GUYANA

Rockstone
Linden

PARAMARIBO

Nieuw
Amsterdam
St.-Laurent-
du-Maroni
Sinnamary

Kourou

Guiana
Highlands

W.J. van
Blommesteinmeer
Kabalebo
Reservoir

SURINAM

Cayenne

French
Guiana
(France)

Acarai Mts.

Equator 0°

BRAZIL

Amazon

60°

39

PERU, BOLIVIA & NORTH BRAZIL

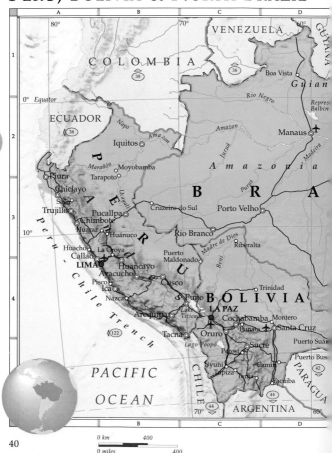

VENEZUELA

COLOMBIA

GUYANA

Guian

Boa Vista

Rio Negro

Repres
Balbin

Equator

ECUADOR

Napo

Amazon

Manaus

Iquitos

Marañón

Moyobamba

Tarapoto

Amazon

Amazonia

Purús

BRA

Piura

Chiclayo

Sa

Trujillo

Ucayali

Cruzeiro do Sul

Porto Velho

Pucallpa

Chimbote

Huaraz

Huánuco

Rio Branco

Madre de Dios

Riberalta

Huacho

La Oroya

Callao

LIMA

Huancayo

Ayacucho

Puerto
Maldonado

Beni

Pisco

Ica

Cusco

Trinidad

Nazca

Puno

BOLIVIA

Arequipa

Lake
Titicaca

LA PAZ

Cochabamba

Montero

Tacna

Oruro

Punata

Santa Cruz

Lago Poopó

Puerto Suár

Potosí

Sucre

Puerto Bus

Uyuni

Camir

PARAGUA

Tupiza

Tarija

Yacuiba

CHILE

ARGENTINA

PACIFIC

OCEAN

Peru-Chile Trench

0 km   400

0 miles   400

SURINAM

French Guiana *(France)*

ATLANTIC

OCEAN

Highlands

Macapá

Ilha Caviana

Amazon

Santarém

Ilha de Marajó

Belém

São Luís

Paranaíba

Equator 0°

Ilha Fernando de Noronha

Xingu

Represa de Tucuruí

Imperatriz

Teresina

Fortaleza

Mossoró

Z I L

Carolina

Juàzeiro do Norte

Campina Grande

Natal

João Pessoa

tes Pires

Araguaia

Tocantins

Represa de Sobradinho

São Francisco

Juàzeiro

Recife

Palmas

Maceió

10°

Aracaju

Planalto de Mato Grosso

Taguatinga

Feira de Santana

Brazilian

Salvador

Cuiabá

Anápolis

BRASÍLIA

Highlands

Itabuna

Goiânia

Vitória da Conquista

Montes Claros

Governador Valadares

Campo Grande

Uberlândia

Abrolhos Bank

Hotspur Seamount

Uberaba

Divinópolis

Belo Horizonte

Paraná

Ribeirão Preto

Vitória

Marília

Nova Iguaçu

Campos

20°

Londrina

Campinas

Sorocaba

Taubaté

Juiz de Fora

Rio de Janeiro

São Paulo

Tropic of Capricorn

PARAGUAY, URUGUAY & SOUTH BRAZIL

0 km 200

0 miles 200

ZIL

erlândia

40

Governador

Valadares

Abrolhos
Bank

Hotspur
Seamount

Iberaba

Belo Horizonte

ão Grande

Divinópolis

Vitória

Champlaim
Seamount

20°

ranca

Represa de Furnas

Montague
Seamount

Ribeirão Preto

Cachoeiro de
Itapemirim

Vitória
Seamount

Juiz de Fora

Campos

Jaseur
Seamount

Volta Redonda

Campinas

Nova Iguaçu

rocaba

Taubaté

Rio de Janeiro

São Paulo

Santos

Tropic of Capricorn

Santos
Plateau

ATLANTIC

46

OCEAN

30°

Rio
Grande
Rise

Argentine

Basin

40°

E   F   G

CHILE & ARGENTINA

44

0 km 200

0 miles 200

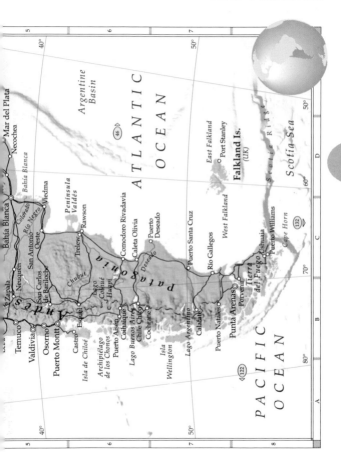

THE ATLANTIC OCEAN

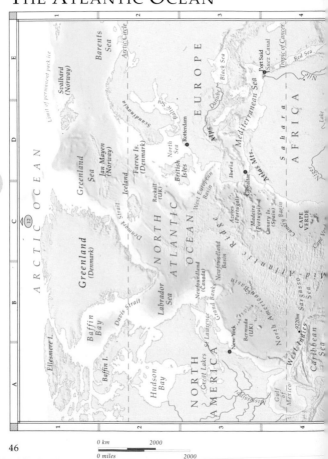

E

Barents Sea

Svalbard (Norway)

Limit of permanent pack ice

Arctic Circle

EUROPE

Port Said

Suez Canal

Tropic of Cancer

Red Sea

Black Sea

Danube

Baltic Sea

Scandinavia

Alps

Mediterranean Sea

Atlas Mts.

Sahara

AFRICA

Lake

D

Greenland Sea

Jan Mayen (Norway)

Iceland

Faeroe Is. (Denmark)

North Sea

Rotterdam

British Isles

Rockall (UK)

Iberia

Gibraltar

C

ARCTIC OCEAN

Denmark Strait

NORTH ATLANTIC OCEAN

West European Basin

Azores (Portugal)

Madeira (Portugal)

Canary Is. (Spain)

CAPE VERDE

Cape Verde

Greenland (Denmark)

B

Ellesmere I.

Baffin I.

Baffin Bay

Davis Strait

Labrador Sea

Newfoundland (Canada)

Newfoundland Basin

Grand Banks

Bermuda (UK)

North American Basin

Mid-Atlantic Ridge

9220m

Sargasso Sea

A

Hudson Bay

NORTH AMERICA

Great Lakes

St Lawrence

New York

Mississippi

Gulf of Mexico

West Indies

Caribbean Sea

1   2   3   4

0 km   2000

0 miles   2000

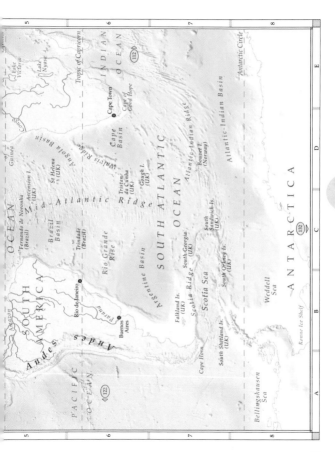

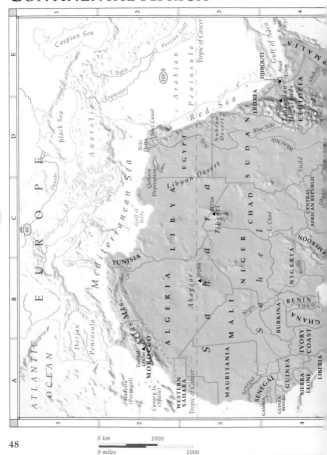

Caspian Sea

Persian Gulf

Tropic of Cancer

Gulf of Aden

DJIBOUTI

L. Assad
-155m

SOMALIA

Black Sea

Tigris

Euphrates

Arabian Peninsula

Red Sea

ERITREA

Shabell

ETHIOPIA

Ethiopian Highlands

EUROPE

Danube

Anatolia

Suez Canal

Nile Delta

Nile

Nubian Desert

Blue Nile

White Nile

SUDAN

Sudd

Mediterranean Sea

Gulf of Sirte

EGYPT

Qattara Depression

Libyan Desert

S a h a r a

Tibesti ▲3415m

CHAD

L. Chad

CENTRAL AFRICAN REPUBLIC

TUNISIA

ALGERIA

LIBYA

NIGER

CAMEROON

Benue

NIGERIA

Atlas Mts.

Ahaggar ▲2918m

S a h e l

BENIN

TOGO

GHANA

Toubkal ▲
4165m

MOROCCO

MALI

BURKINA

Niger

IVORY COAST

ATLANTIC OCEAN

Iberian Peninsula

Madeira (Portugal)

Canary Is. (Spain)

WESTERN SAHARA

Tropic of Cancer

MAURITANIA

SENEGAL

Senegal

GAMBIA

GUINEA BISSAU

GUINEA

SIERRA LEONE

LIBERIA

0 km   1000

0 miles   1000

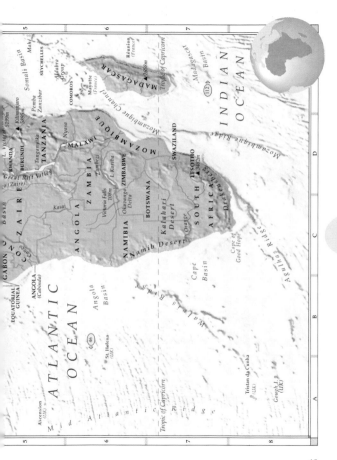

ATLANTIC OCEAN

INDIAN OCEAN

Mid-Atlantic Ridge

Tropic of Capricorn

MADAGASCAR

Tropic of Capricorn

Mozambique Ridge

Agulhas Ridge

Walvis Ridge

Cape Basin

Angola Basin

Somali Basin

Madagascar Basin

Mozambique Channel

Great Rift Valley

Congo (Zaire) Basin

SEYCHELLES

COMOROS

Réunion (France)

Mayotte (France)

Aldabra Group

Mahé

Pemba

Zanzibar

TANZANIA

RWANDA

BURUNDI

ZAIRE

CONGO

GABON

EQUATORIAL GUINEA

ANGOLA (Cabinda)

ANGOLA

NAMIBIA

ZAMBIA

MALAWI

MOZAMBIQUE

ZIMBABWE

BOTSWANA

SWAZILAND

LESOTHO

SOUTH AFRICA

Namib Desert

Kalahari Desert

Victoria Falls 108m

Okavango Delta

Drakensberg 3482m

Cape of Good Hope

L. Victoria 5199m

Kilimanjaro 5895m

L. Tanganyika

L. Nyasa

L. Kariba

Zambezi

Kasai

Congo

Orange

Ascension (UK)

St. Helena (UK)

Tristan da Cunha (UK)

Gough I. (UK)

46

112

NORTHWEST AFRICA

0 km 400

0 miles 400

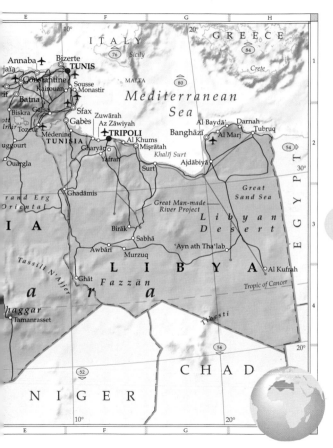

ITALY
GREECE
Sicily
Crete
MALTA
Mediterranean Sea

Annaba
jaïa
Bizerte
TUNIS
Constantine
Kairouan
Sousse
Monastir
if
Batna
Biskra
Gafsa
Sfax
ott
Tozeur
Gabès
Zuwārah
Az Zāwiyah
TRIPOLI
Al Khums
Mişrātah
Al Baydā'
Darnah
uggourt
Médenine
TUNISIA
Gharyān
Banghāzī
Al Marj
Tubruq
Ouargla
Yafran
Khalīj Surt
Ajdābiyā
Surt

rand Erg
Oriental
Ghadāmis
Great Man-made
River Project
Great
Sand Sea

Libyan
Desert

IA
Birāk
Sabhā
'Ayn ath Tha'lab

Tassili N'ajjer
a
Awbārī
Murzuq

haggar
Tamanrasset
Ghāt
Fazzān
a
LIBYA
Al Kufrah

Tropic of Cancer

EGYPT

Tibesti

NIGER
CHAD

51

ATLANTIC OCEAN

WESTERN SAHARA
(occupied by Morocco)

Tropic of Cancer

Zouérat

Nouâdhibou

Râs
Nouâdhibou

Atâr

S

MAURITANIA

NOUAKCHOTT

L. Rkiz
Rosso
Aleg
Kiffa
Saint-Louis
Senegal
Kaédi

CAPE VERDE

PRAIA

DAKAR
Thiès
Diourbel
SENEGAL
Kaolack
Kayes
GAMBIA
BANJUL
Georgetown
Ziguinchor
Kolda
BISSAU
Bafatá
GUINEA-BISSAU

Nioro

Ségou

BAMAK

Labé
Siguiri
Bougouni
Sika

GUINEA

Kindia
Kankan
Korh

CONAKRY
Odienné
IVOI
COAS

FREETOWN
Makeni
Bo
SIERRA LEONE
Nzérékoré
Kenema

Bouak
Man
Dalo

Tubmanburg
MONROVIA
YAMOUSSOUKRO

ATLANTIC OCEAN

Buchanan
Zwedru
Gagnoa

LIBERIA

Harper

Buyo R

20°

10°

52

0 km   250

0 miles   250

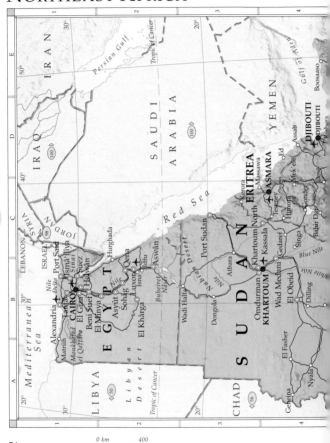

0 km   400

0 miles   400

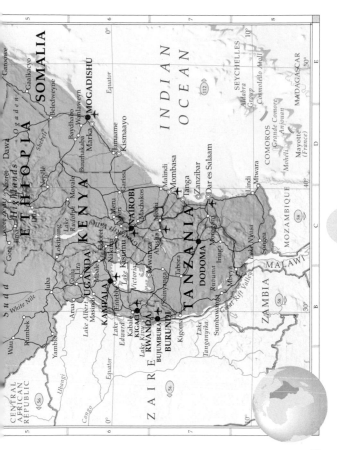

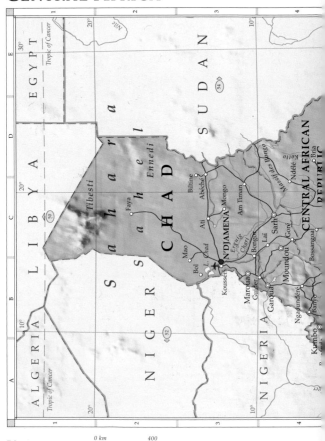

0 km 400

0 miles 400

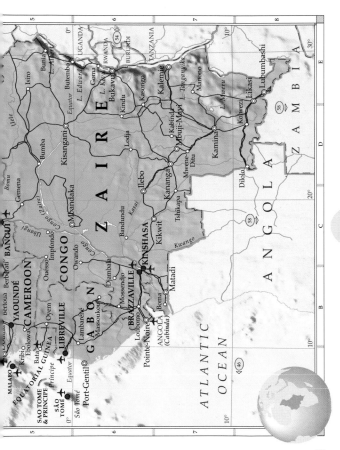

A map of Southern Africa showing countries including Angola, Zambia, Namibia, Botswana, Zimbabwe, South Africa, and Lesotho, with the Atlantic Ocean to the west.

Labels on the map include:

Cabinda (Angola), Cabinda, Ambriz, Uíge, LUANDA, N'Dalatando, Lucapa, Saurimo, Malanje, Congo, ZAIRE, Lake Tanganyika, Ndola, Mufulira, Sumbe, Lobito, Benguela, Huambo, Menongue, Zambezi, Chingola, Kitwe, Luanshya, ZAMBIA, LUSAKA, Choma, Lake Kariba, Lubango, Namibe, Tombua, N'Giva, Okavango, Cuito, Cunene, Livingstone, Chitungwi, ZIMBA, Ondangwa, Etosha Pan, Rundu, Tsumeb, Grootfontein, Okavango Delta, Maun, Makgadikgadi, Bulawayo, Francistown, NAMIBIA, Ghanzi, BOTSWANA, Okahandja, WINDHOEK, Kalahari, Mahalapye, Limpopo, Swakopmund, Walvis Bay, Rehoboth, GABORONE, PRETORI, Lobatse, Mmabatho, Soweto, Johannesburg, Keetmanshoop, Desert, Lüderitz, Karasburg, Kimberley, Vaal, Kroons, Orange R., Bloemfontein, MASER, SOUTH AFRICA, LESOTHO, Middelburg, Beaufort West, Oudtshoorn, East Lon, Bellville, Cape Town, Port Elizabeth, Cape of Good Hope, Cape Basin, ATLANTIC OCEAN, Skeleton Coast, Namib, Tropic of Capricorn, Fish

10°, 20°, 30°, 20°, Tropic of Capricorn, 30°, 0°, 10°, 20°

0 km   400
0 miles   400

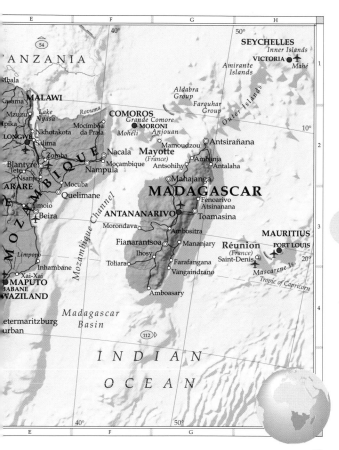

TANZANIA

Mbala

MALAWI

Kasama
Mzuzu
Lake
Nyasa
Ipika
LONGWE
Nkhotakota
Salima
Zomba
Blantyre
Teto
Nsanje
ARARE
Mocuba
Chimoio
Beira
Limpopo
Inhambane
MAPUTO
BABANE
WAZILAND
etermaritzburg
urban

Rovuma
Mocímboa
da Praia
Nacala
Moçambique
Nampula
Quelimane
Mozambique Channel

MOZAMBIQUE

COMOROS
Grande Comore
MORONI
Mohéli
Anjouan

Aldabra
Group
Farquhar
Group

SEYCHELLES
Inner Islands
VICTORIA ● Mahé

Amirante
Islands

Outer Islands

Mamoudzou
Mayotte
(France)
Antsohihy

Antsirañana
Ambanja
Antalaha

Mahajanga

MADAGASCAR

ANTANANARIVO
Morondava
Ambositra
Fianarantsoa
Ihosy
Toliara
Amboasary
Mananjary
Farafangana
Vangaindrano

Fenoarivo
Atsinanana
Toamasina

Réunion
(France)
Saint-Denis

MAURITIUS
PORT LOUIS

Mascarene Is.
Tropic of Capricorn

Madagascar
Basin

INDIAN

OCEAN

40°   50°

59

CONTINENTAL EUROPE

ARCTIC OCEAN

Norwegian Basin

Arctic Circle

Norwegian Sea

ICELAND

Faeroe-Iceland Ridge

Faeroe Islands *(Denmark)*

Shetland Is.

2468m▲

NORWAY

Orkney Is.

Kjølen Mts

SWEDE

Outer Hebrides

North Sea

ATLANTIC

UNITED KINGDOM

DENMARK

OCEAN

IRELAND

NETHERLANDS

Elbe

Nort

GERMANY

Thames

BELGIUM

Rhine

English Channel

LUX.

CZEC

RI

FRANCE

Seine

Meuse

Danube

AUSTR

Loire

A   L   P   S

SWITZ.

LIECH.

SLOVEN

Biscay Plain

1886m▲

Massif

Mont

Blanc

4807m

ITALY

Adri

Bay of Biscay

Central

MONACO

SAN MARINO

C. Finisterre

Garonne

3404m

ANDORRA

Corsica

VATICAN CITY

Pyrenees

Apenni

Tyrrhenian

PORTUGAL

SPAIN

Balearic Is.

Sardinia

Sea

Guadalquivir

Etna

3369r

C. St Vincent

Mulhacén

▲3478m

Mediterranean Sea

Sicil

Gibraltar *(UK)*

MALTA

AFRICA

60

0 km   600

0 miles   600

North Cape

Barents Sea

Lapland
317m

Kola
Peninsula

Arctic Circle

White Sea

Gulf of Bothnia

FINLAND

N. Dvina

Ural Mountains

Gulf of Finland

Baltic Sea

ESTONIA

RUSSIAN FEDERATION

LATVIA

Volga

Dvina

92

LITHUANIA

USSIAN FED.
Kaliningrad)

uropean

Plain

POLAND

BELORUSSIA

Vistula

Pripet
Marshes

UKRAINE

Dnieper

Don

Volga

LOVAKIA

Carpathians

MOLDAVIA

UNGARY

Sea of
Azov

Volga
Delta
-28m

Aral
Sea

ROATIA

ROMANIA

Danube

Black

Caucasus Mts.

OS. &
ERZ.

YUGO.

Balkan Mts.

Sea

El'brus 5642m

Caspian
Sea

MAC.

BULGARIA

a

LBANIA

Pindus
Mts.

Aegean
Sea

an
Sea

GREECE

A

S

I

A

Tigris

Euphrates

92

Crete

THE NORTH ATLANTIC

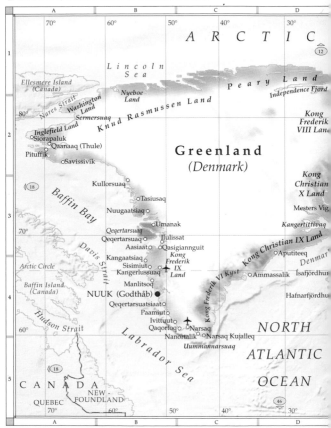

A R C T I C

Lincoln Sea

Ellesmere Island (Canada)

Nyeboe Land

P e a r y   L a n d

Independence Fjord

Nares Strait

Washington Land

Kong Frederik VIII Land

Sermersuaq

Knud Rasmussen Land

Inglefield Land

Siorapaluk

Qaanaaq (Thule)

Pituffik

Savissivik

G r e e n l a n d

(Denmark)

Kong Christian X Land

Kullorsuaq

Mesters Vig

Baffin Bay

Tasiusaq

Nuugaatsiaq

Kangertittivaq

Umanak

Qeqertarsuaq

Ilulissat

Qeqertarsuaq

Aasiaat

Qasigiannguit

Kong Christian IX Land

Davis Strait

Kangaatsiaq

Kong Frederik IX Land

Aputiteeq

Denmar

Sisimiut

Arctic Circle

Kangerlussuaq

Ammassalik

Ísafjördhu

Baffin Island (Canada)

Manlitsoq

Kong Frederik VI Kyst

Hafnarfjördhu

NUUK (Godthåb)

Qeqertarsuatsiaato

Paamiut

NORTH

Hudson Strait

Ivittuut

Qaqortoq

Narsaq

Nanortalik

Narsaq Kujalleq

ATLANTIC

Uummannarsuaq

Labrador Sea

OCEAN

C A N A D A

NEW-FOUNDLAND

QUEBEC

0 km   500

0 miles   500

OCEAN

Wandel Sea

Greenland Sea

Svalbard
(Norway) *Nordaustlandet*

Spitsbergen *Pyramiden*

Barentsburg○ ○Longyearbyen

Edgeøya

○Danmarkshavn

Greenland Basin

○Daneborg

Mohns Ridge

Jan Mayen
(Norway)

North Cape

○toqqortoormiit

Norwegian Sea

○Húsavík

○kureyri ○Seydhisfjördhur

EYKJAVÍK○ Djúpivogur

elfoss○

ICELAND

vyville-Thomson Ridge

Shetland
(UK)

Orkney
(UK)

Hebrides
(UK)

68

**UNITED
KINGDOM**

IRELAND

Faeroe Islands
(Denmark)

○Tórshavn

NORWAY

SWEDEN

64

FINLAND

ESTONIA

LATVIA

LITH.

66

DENMARK

NETH. GERMANY POLAND

Arctic Circle

80°

70°

60°

20°

10°

0°

10°

20°

SCANDINAVIA & FINLAND

RUSSIAN FEDERATION

Barents Sea

FINLAND

LAPLAND

SWEDEN

NORWAY

ARCTIC OCEAN

Norwegian Sea

North Cape
Hammerfest
Tromsø
Harstad
Lofoten
Bodø
Mo
Steinkjer
Trondheimsfjorden

Vardø
Kirkenes
Sodankylä
Kittilä
Kemijärvi
Rovaniemi
Kemi
Tornio
Oulu
Kuusamo
Kajaani
Kokkola
Skellefteå
Piteå
Luleå
Gällivare
Kiruna
Narvik

Arctic Circle

70°
65°
35°
30°
25°
20°
15°
10°
5°
0°

0 km   150

0 miles   150

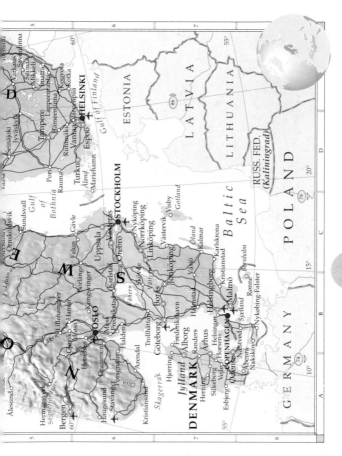

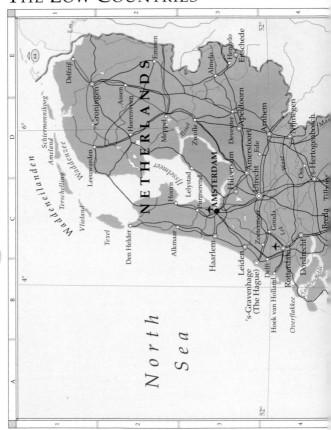

0 km   50

0 miles   50

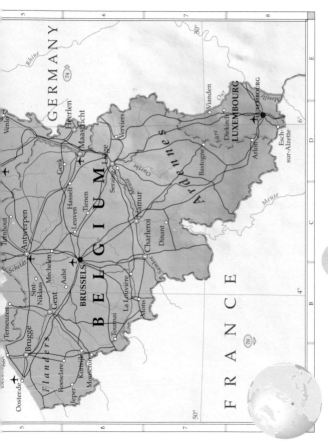

GERMANY

Rhine

Venlo

Heerlen

Maastricht

Genk

Hasselt

Leuven

Tienen

Antwerpen

Turnhout

Mechelen

Aalst

BRUSSELS

Sint-
Niklaas

Gent

Terneuzen

Brugge

Oostende

Roeselare

Kortrijk

Mouscron

Ieper

Flanders

Scheldt

BELGIUM

Tournai

Mons

La Louvière

Charleroi

Dinant

Namur

Sambre

Meuse

Liège

Seraing

Verviers

Ourthe

Ardennes

Bastogne

Sûre

Diekirch

Vianden

Our

LUXEMBOURG

LUXEMBOURG

Arlon

Esch-
sur-Alzette

Moselle

Meuse

FRANCE

50°

50°

0 km   100

0 miles   100

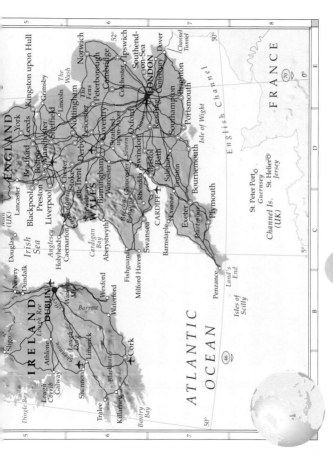

Administrative border

FRANCE & ANDORRA

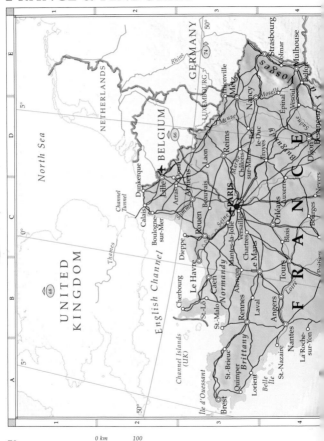

0 km   100

0 miles   100

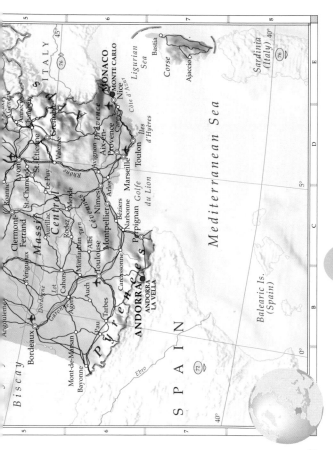

SPAIN & PORTUGAL

0 km 100

0 miles 100

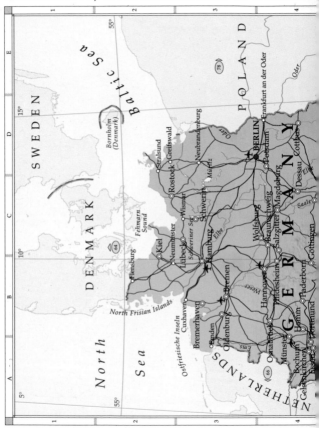

74

0 km   100

0 miles   100

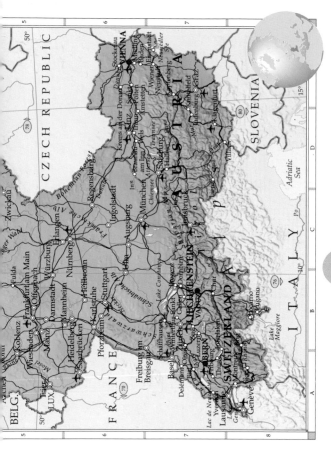

ITALY & MALTA

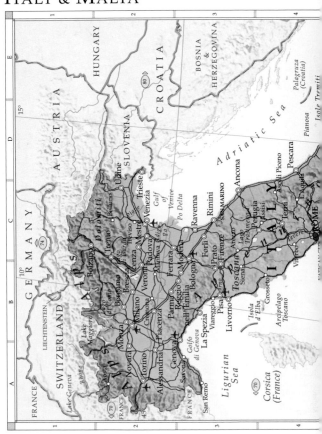

0 km   100

0 miles   100

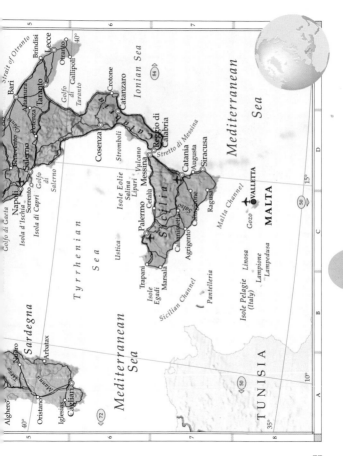

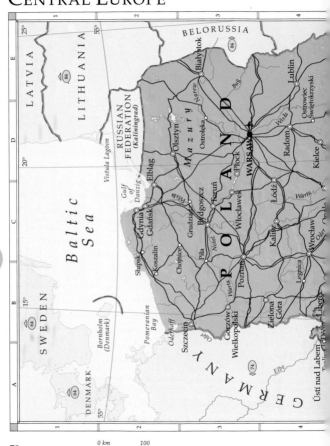

0 km 100

0 miles 100

THE WESTERN BALKANS

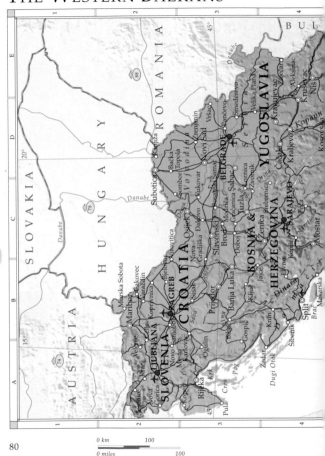

0 km   100

0 miles   100

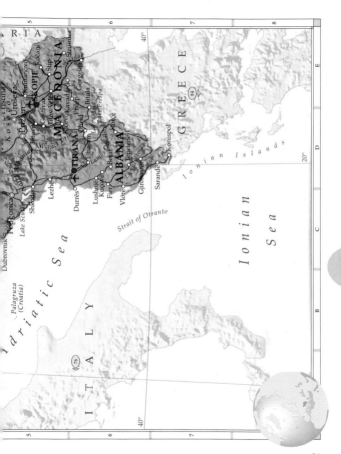

THE MEDITERRANEAN

ATLANTIC OCEAN

English Channel

Thames

Seine

Rhine

Danube

E U

Loire

Bay of Biscay

Dordogne

Garonne

Massif Central

Rhône

Mt. Blanc 4807m

L. Geneva

Alps Alps

Po

Genoa

Apennine

Marseille

Livorno

C. Finisterre

Pyrenees 3404m

Ebro

Golfe du Lion

Corsica

Napl

Iberian

Tagus

Valencia

Barcelona

Balearic Is.

Sardinia

Tyrrhen Sea

Peninsula

Guadalquivir

3478m

Med it

C. St Vincent

Gibraltar

Oran

Algiers

Tell Atlas

2328m

Tunis

M

Strait of Gibraltar

Rif

Atlas Mountains

Chott el Jerid

Sfax

Tripoli

Canary Is. (Spain)

4165m

Grand Erg Occidental

Grand Erg Oriental

A F R I

S a h a r

0 km   400

0 miles   400

Europe

60

2653m▲ Carpathians

Hungarian Plain

2303m▲

Dnieper

Don

2543m▲

Danube Delta

Crimea

Sea of Azov

Caucasus Mts.

El'brus 5642m

Danube

Black Sea

Dinaric Alps

2693m▲ Balkan Mts. 2376m
2925m▲

Bosporus

Rhodope Mts.
Pindus Mts.

Adriatic Sea

Mt. Ararat ▲ 5122m

Ionian Sea

Lesbos
Aegean Sea

Izmir

Anatolia

3917m▲

Lake Van

Piraeus

Peloponnese

Sicily

Kos

Taurus Mts.

Rhodes

Crete

Cyprus

3088m▲

Euphrates

Tigris

Mediterranean Sea

878m▲

Haifa

Anti-Lebanon

Syrian Desert

Gulf of Sirte

Nile Delta

Port Said

Dead Sea -400m

92

Qattara Depression -133m

Suez Canal

ASIA

AFRICA

Nile

Red Sea

Arabian Peninsula

Libyan Desert

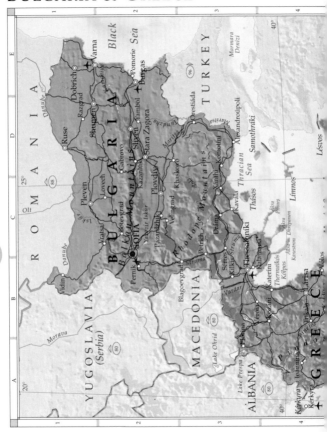

0 km   100

0 miles   100

TURKEY

96

Ródos

Kárpathos

Ródos

Dodekánisos

Sámos

Kos

Chíos ●Chíos

Ikaria

Astypálaia

Aegean
Sea

Tínos

Míkonos

Náxos

Amorgós

Íos

Ándros

Thíra

Páros

Sea of Crete

54

Irákleio

K y k l á d e s

25°

Kéa

Mírtôo Pelagos

Mílos

Sea of Crete

Kríti

Chalkída

ATHENS

Piraiévs

Achárnai

Diavriga

Karínthou

Chaniá

Mediterranean Sea

Corinth

Kórinthos

Kórinthos

Náfplio

Korinthiakós Kólpos

Egaleo

Lívadiá

Pátra

P e l o p ó n n i s o s

Spárti

Kjthíra

50

Agrínio

Pátra

Kalamáta

LIBYA

Kefallinía

Zákynthos

Nísoi

Ionian
Sea

76

35°

35°

20°

THE BALTIC STATES & BELORUSSIA

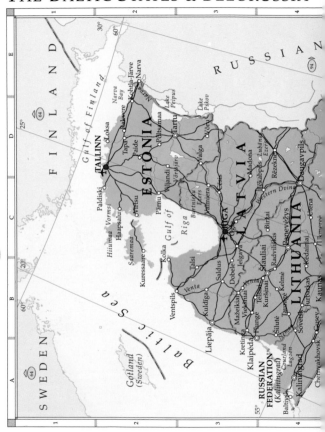

0 km   100

0 miles   100

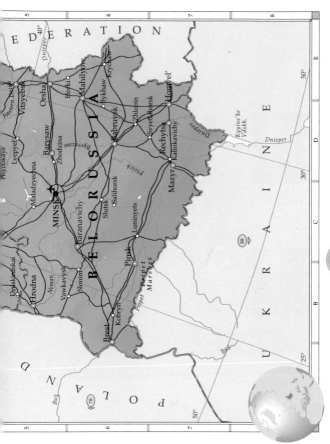

0 km   100

0 miles   100

0 km   400

0 miles   400

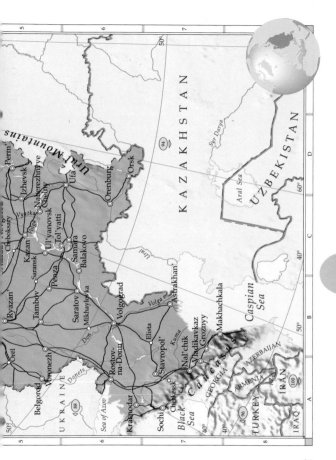

CONTINENTAL NORTH & WEST ASIA

ARCTIC OCEAN

Franz Josef Land

Svalbard
(Norway)

Novaya Zemlya

Kara
Sea

Barents
Sea

Yamal
Peninsula

Arctic Circle

RUSSIAN F

Ural Mts. Ob'

West Siberian
Plain

Baltic
Sea

North European Plain

Central Russian
Upland

Volga

Don

Volga

KAZAKHSTAN

Kirghiz
Steppe

Kazakh
Uplands

L. Balkhash

Altai Mts.

S

Ob'

Danube

Black Sea

Caucasus Mts.

AZERBAIJAN

GEORGIA

ARMENIA

Syr Darya

Aral
Sea Kyzyl Kum

UZBEKISTAN

Tien Shan

Pik Pobedy 7439m

Bosporus

Dardanelles

TURKEY

Mt. Ararat

Caspian
Sea

TURKMENISTAN

Kara Kum

Amu Darya

KYRGYZSTAN

Communism Peak 7495m

TAJIKISTAN

Mediterranean
Sea

CYPRUS
LEBANON
ISRAEL

Tigris

Euphrates

SYRIA

Syrian
Desert

5604m

IRAN

Iranian
Plateau

AFGHANISTAN

Hindu Kush

A

S

Dead Sea
-400m

JORDAN

IRAQ

KUWAIT

An Nafud

BAHRAIN

QATAR

Zagros Mts.

Persian Gulf

Gulf of Oman

Indus

Brahmaputra

104

Suez Canal

Tropic of Cancer

Nile

Red Sea

Arabian Peninsula

SAUDI
ARABIA

U.A.E.

OMAN

60

48

Rub' al Khali

Arabian
Sea

Bay
of
Bengal

AFRICA

YEMEN

Gulf of Aden

Socotra
(Yemen)

0 km   1000

0 miles   1000

ARCTIC OCEAN

naya Zemlya

ymyr insula

Laptev Sea

New Siberian Islands

Limit of permanent pack-ice

East Siberian Sea

Wrangel I.

ral Siberian Plateau

Chukchi Sea

e r i a

Cherskiy Range

Arctic Circle

Bering Strait

E R A T I O N

Verkhoyansk Range

Lena

Kolyma Range

Lena

Sea of Okhotsk

Kamchatka
▲4,750m

Bering Sea

Stanovoy Range

Dzhugdzhur Range

L. Baikal

Amur

Aleutian Islands (USA)

Sikhote-Alin Range

Sakhalin

Sea of Japan

Hokkaidō

Honshū

PACIFIC

r River

OCEAN

Yangtze

Kyūshū

Hawaiian Is. (USA)

Tropic of Cancer

Taiwan

Hainan Dao

South China Sea

Luzon

Northern Marianas (USA)

Mariana Trench

Guam (USA)

RUSSIA & KAZAKHSTAN

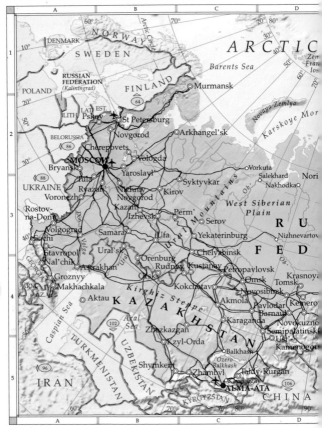

0 km   500

0 miles   500

TURKEY, CYPRUS & THE CAUCASUS

0 km   200

0 miles   200

THE NEAR EAST

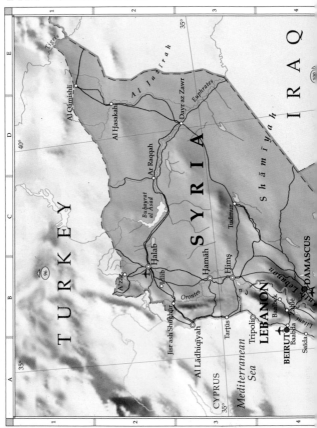

0 km   100

0 miles   100

West Bank

Irbid
Al Mafraq
Az Zarqā
Petah
Nāblus
Herzliyya
AMMAN
Tel Aviv-Yafo
Jericho
Holon
JERUSALEM
Bethlehem
Dead
Gaza
Sea
ISRAEL
JORDAN
Gaza Strip
Be'ér Sheva
Al Karak
Petra
At Tafilah
Ha Negev
Ma'ān
Elat
Al 'Aqabah
EGYPT
Gulf of Aqaba
Gulf of Suez
Red Sea

SAUDI ARABIA

30°

35°

30°

100

54

OCCUPIED TERRITORIES

The West Bank, Gaza Strip and Golan Heights have been occupied by Israel since the Six Day War in 1967.

Palestinians gained home rule of the Gaza Strip and Jericho in 1994.

99

THE MIDDLE EAST

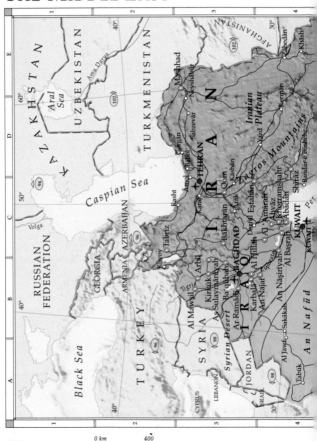

0 km 400

0 miles 400

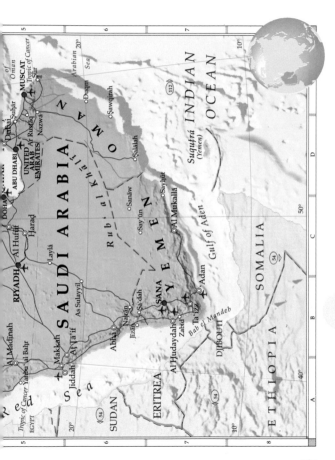

Gulf *of* Oman

Arabian 20°

Arabian Sea

MUSCAT

Dabā Şuḥār

Tropic of Cancer

Şīr

ABU DHABI

oDuqm

oŞawqirah

UNITED
ARAB Ar Rustāq
EMIRATES Nazwā

O M A N

Salālah

112

INDIAN OCEAN

DOHA

Suqutrā
(Yemen)

Al Hufūf

Harad

R u b ' a l K h ā l ī

RIYADH

Laylā

oŞan'āw'

oSayḥūt

Al Mukallā

S A U D I A R A B I A

As Sulayyil

oSay'ūn

Y E M E N

Gulf of Aden

50°

Al Madīnah

Ṭaraf

Sa'dah

Yanbu'al Baḥr

Abhā

Makkah

Jīzān

SANA

Ta'izz

Adan

S O M A L I A

54

Jiddah

At Ţā'if

Zabīd

Al Ḥudaydah

Bāb el Mandeb

R e d S e a

Tropic of Cancer

20°

ERITREA

DJIBOUTI

E T H I O P I A

EGYPT

SUDAN

54

40°

10°

54

101

CENTRAL ASIA

0 km   200

0 miles   200

A Z A K H S T A N

Lake Balkhash

94

70°   80°

Kara-Balta   **BISHKEK**   Tyup
Talas   Tokmak   Karakol
Issyk-Kul'   Ozero Issyk-Kul'

HKENT Chirchik   **KYRGYZSTAN**   Tien Shan
Angren   Namangan   Naryn
Almalyk   Andizhan   Dzhalal-Abad   Naryn
hudzhand   Kokand   Qsh   Kokshaal-Tau
Tyube   Fergana
Sukyuka   Khaydarkan
Zeravshan sarkhob
USHANBE   **TAJIKSTAN**   40°

Nurek   Dangara   Bartang   Murgab   C H I N A
ungan
yube   Kulyab   Khorog   106
nez   Parkhar   Pamir
olm   Feyzabad   Pamirs
Kunduz   Indus
Baghlan   Aksai Chin
honru   Occupied by China,
arikar   Asadabad   claimed by India.
BUL   Jalalabad

Ghazni   Gardez   Jammu & Kashmir   Demchok/Dêmqog
A "line of control" was agreed   Claimed by India
between India and Pakistan in   and China.
1972.

A K I S T A N   I N D I A

70°   114

E   F   G

103

EAST & SOUTH ASIA

A · S · I · A

Aral Sea

Lake Baikal

92

MONGOLIA

Altai Mountains

4362m

Gobi

Caspian
Sea

Tien Shan

7439m

Turpan Depression
-154m

Takla Makan

Altun Mts.

CHINA

Iranian
Plateau

Hindu Kush

K2
8611m

Kunlun Mts.

Great Wall
of China

Himalayas

Plateau of Tibet

Yangtze

PAKISTAN

NEPAL

BHUTAN

Hong Kong
(UK)

Indus

Thar
Desert

Mt Everest
8848m

Ganges Plain

Ganges

BANGLADESH

Macao
(Portugal)

Tropic of Cancer

Indus
Delta

INDIA

Ganges
Delta

BURMA

Irrawaddy

Salween

Mekong

Hainan
Dao

VIETNA

Arabian
Peninsula

Arabian
Sea

Godavari

Deccan

Western Ghats

Eastern Ghats

Bay
of
Bengal

THAILAND

LAOS

Sauth
Chin
Sea

48

Lakshadweep
(India)

Andaman Is.
(India)

Andaman
Sea

Gulf
of
Thailand

CAMBOD

4101

MALDIVES

SRI
LANKA

Nicobar Is.
(India)

MALAYSIA

BRUNE

Equator

SINGAPORE

Borne

112

Sumatra

3800m

IND

INDIAN
OCEAN

Krakatau
813m

Java Se

Java

Bali

Str. of Malacca

Java Trench

0 km   1000

0 miles   1000

Sea of Okhotsk

Aleutian Islands (USA)

Sakhalin

Amur

Manchurian Plain

Kurile Is.

Kurile Trench

Emperor Seamounts

NORTH KOREA

Sea of Japan

Hokkaidō

SOUTH KOREA

llow Sea

Honshū

JAPAN

▲Mt. Fuji 3776m

Hawaiian Islands (USA)

Korea Strait

East China Sea

Kyūshū

Honshu Ridge

Ryukyu Islands (Japan)

Tropic of Cancer

AIWAN

- Luzon Strait

Northern Marianas Is. (USA)

122

PACIFIC

OCEAN

Marshall Islands

Guam (USA)

Micronesia

Mariana Trench

PHILIPPINES

Caroline Islands

Melanesia

Equator

ebes Sea

Moluccas ebes

5030m

Bismarck Archipelago

E S I A

Band a Sea

New Guinea

res

Timor

Arafura Sea

Solomon Islands

Timor Sea

124

AUSTRALASIA

WESTERN CHINA & MONGOLIA

0 km   400

0 miles   400

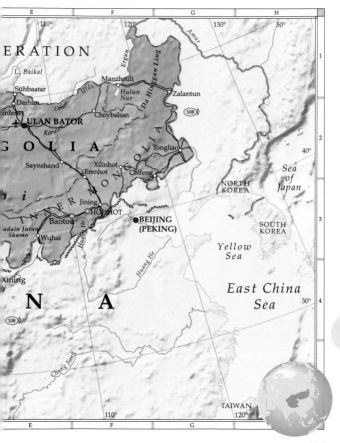

110°   120°   130°   50°

ERATION

L. Baikal

Sühbaatar

Darhan

Erdenet

ULAN BATOR

GOLIA

Saynshand

Xilinhot
Erenhot

Jining

Baotou
HOHHOT

Wuhai

Xining

N   A

Manzhouli

Hulun
Nur

Ergun

Amur

Uldz

Onon

Choybalsan

Kerulen

Da Hinggan Ling

TIAN ER (SHAN)

Huang He

Zalantun

(108)

Tongliao

Chifeng

**BEIJING
(PEKING)**

NORTH
KOREA

SOUTH
KOREA

Yellow
Sea

East China
Sea

Sea
of
Japan

40°

30°

adain Jaran
Shamo

(108)

Chang Jiang

110°   120°

TAIWAN

Great Wall of China

EASTERN CHINA & KOREA

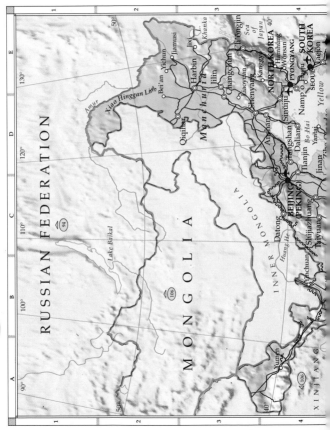

0 km 400

0 miles 400

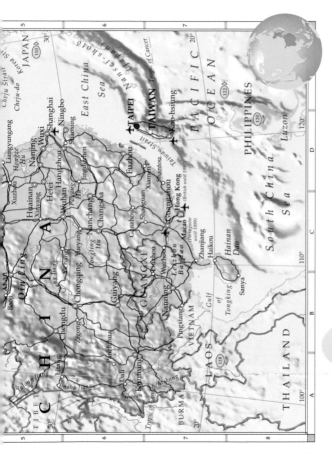

Great Wall of China

JAPAN

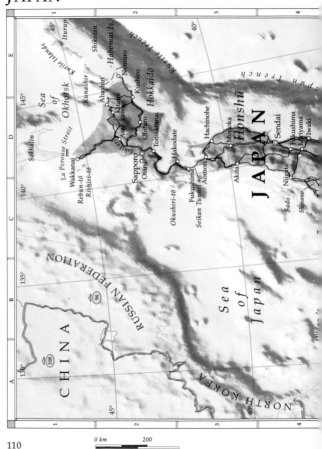

0 km   200

0 miles   200

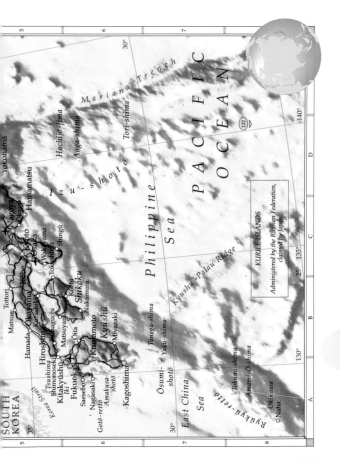

SOUTH
KOREA

Matsue
Hamada
Tsushima
Shimonoseki
Kitakyūshū
Iki
Fukuoka
Saseho
Nagasaki
Gotō-rettō

Tottori
Okayama
Kurashiki
Yamaguchi
Ōita
Kumamoto
Amakusa-
shotō
Kagoshima

Kōbe
Ōsaka
Wakayama
Kōchi
Shikoku
Nakamura
Kyūshū
Miyazaki

Kyōto
Nagoya
Okazaki
Hamamatsu
Tsu
Shingū
Toba

Yokohama

Izu-shotō

Hachijō-jima
Aoga-shima

Tori-shima

Mariana Trench

PACIFIC
OCEAN

Philippine
Sea

Kyushu-Palau Ridge

⟨122⟩◁

Tanega-shima
Yaku-shima
Ōsumi-
shotō

East China
Sea

Tokuno-shima
Amami-Ō-shima
Oki-awa
Ō-Naha
Ryūkyū-rettō

Korea Strait

KURILE ISLANDS
*Administered by the Russian Federation,
claimed by Japan.*

111

THE INDIAN OCEAN

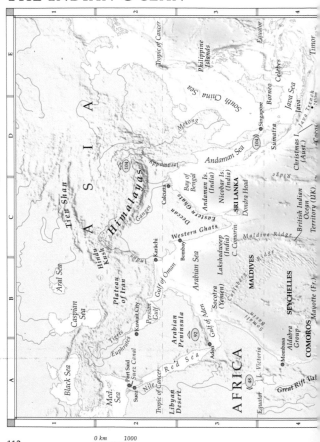

112

0 km   1000

0 miles   1000

Desert
Tropic of Capricorn
AUSTRALIA
(124)
Nullarbor Plain
North West C
Fremantle
Cape
Leeuwin

West
Australia
Basin

Southeast Indian Ridge

South Indian Basin

Wilkes Land

Ninety

Broken Ridge

d-Indian Ridge

INDIAN OCEAN

Kerguelen (Fr.)
Heard I. (Aust.)
Kerguelen Plateau
Macdonald Is. (Aust.)

Crozet Basin

Crozet Is. (Fr.)

MAURITIUS
Mascarene
Plateau

Madagascar
Basin

Tarangana

MADAGASCAR

Madagascar
Ridge

Southwest Indian Ridge

Prince
Edward Is.
(SA)

Atlantic-Indian Basin

Amery Ice
Shelf
(132)

ANTARCTICA

Queen Maud Land

Tropic of Capricorn

Drakensberg

Durban

113

NORTH INDIA, PAKISTAN & BANGLADES

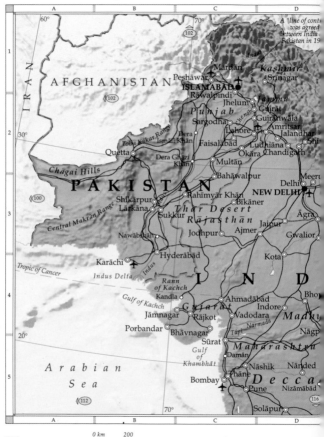

A 'line of cont
was agreed
between India
Pakistan in 19

AFGHANISTAN

IRAN

60°

70°

102

102

100

Toba Kakar Range

Quetta

Chāgai Hills

PAKISTAN

Central Makrān Range

Shikārpur

Lārkāna

Sukkur

Nawābshāh

Karāchi

Indus Delta

Tropic of Cancer

Arabian Sea

112

20°

30°

Peshāwar

Mardān

Kashmīr

ISLAMABAD

Srinagar

Rāwalpindi

Jhelum

Jammu

Gujrāt

Punjab

Gujrānwāla

Sargodha

Lahore

Amritsar

Jalandhar

Shi

Dera
Ismāīl Khān

Faisalābād

Ludhiāna

Dera Ghāzi
Khān

Okāra

Chandīgarh

Multān

NEW DELHI

Delhi

Meeru

Bahāwalpur

Rahīmyār Khān

Bīkaner

Thar Desert

Āgra

Rajasthān

Jaipur

Gwalior

Jodhpur

Ajmer

Kota

Hyderābād

Indus

*Rann
of Kachch*

Gulf of Kachch

Kandla

Ahmadābād

Bho

Gujarāt

Indore

Jāmnagar

Rājkot

Vadodara

Madh

Narmada

Porbandar

Bhāvnagar

Nāgp

Sūrat

Tāpi

I **N** **D**

Damān

Maharashtra

*Gulf
of
Khambhāt*

Nāshik

Nānded

Bombay

Thāne

Decca

Pune

Nizāmābād

116

Solāpur

70°

0 km   200

0 miles   200

XINJIANG

Aksai Chin
occupied by
China, claimed
by India.

Pachok/Dêmqog
owned by
India and China.

QINGHAI

CHINA

106

TIBET

Himalayas

NEPAL

Bareilly
Mpalganj
Uttar
Pradesh
Lucknow
Kānpur
Varanasi
Allahābād
Gaya
Jabalpur
adesh
Bhātāpāra
Raipur
rangal
Warangal

KATHMANDU
Birganj
Gangtok
Biratnagar
Saidpur
Patna
Jamalpur
Rājshāhi
Dhanbād
Rānchi
Bengal
Calcutta
Khulna

Punakha
THIMPHU
BHUTAN

Guwahāti
Dispur
Kohima

Shillong
Sylhet
Imphāl

Brahmaputra

Ganga

West

BANGLADESH

DHAKA

Agartala
Comilla

Āīzawl

BURMA

Tropic of Cancer

118

Chittagong

Ganges Delta

Mahānadi
Cuttack

Orissa

Eastern Ghats

Visākhapatnam

Bay
of
Bengal

IA

Dispur

90°

30°

Tropic of Cancer

20°

90°

- - Ceasefire line

115

SOUTHERN INDIA

Arabian Sea

Arabian Basin

Amīndīvi Is.

Lakshadweep
(India)

Kavaratti I.

Kalpeni I.

Minicoy I.

Thiladhunmathi Atoll

MALDIVES

MALE'

Maldive Ridge

Kolhumadulu Atoll

Huvadhu Atoll

Equator

Thane · Nānded
Bombay · Nizāmābād
Pune · *Decca*
Solāpur
Hyderābā
Belgaum · *Karnātaka*
Pānāji · Hubli
Goa · Dāvangere
Kurnool
Andh
Pra
Bangalore · Vell
Mangalore
Mysore
Tam
Salem · *Na*
Calicut
Coimbatore · Tiruch
Ernākulam · rapp
Cochin · Madur
Kerala · Dhanushk
Trivandrum
Nāgercoil

I N D I

Western Ghats

Krishna

IND

0 km   300
0 miles   300

BURMA

Irrawaddy
Delta

Andaman Is.
(India)

North Andaman

Middle Andaman

Port Blair ○
South Andaman
Little Andaman

Andaman-Nicobar Ridge

*Andaman
Sea*

Nicobar Is.
(India)

Great Nicobar

Sumatra

*B a y
o f
B e n g a l*

Visākhapatnam

Rajahmundry

Vijayawāda

ngole

ellore

Madras

Māmallapuram

ndicherry

alk Strait

affna

SRI LANKA

○Trincomalee
○Batticaloa

Kandy

OLOMBO

alle

Matara

Ceylon Plain

Nineteast Ridge

N OCEAN

Equator

90°

90°

0°

10°

0°

Eastern Ghats

arangal

odāvari

118

120

112

MAINLAND SOUTHEAST ASIA

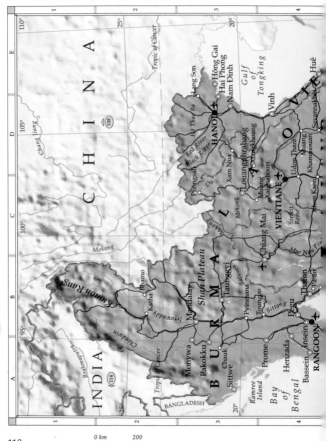

0 km 200

0 miles 200

Quí Nhơn
Nha Trang
Da Lat
Kampong Cham
Hô Chí Minh
Mekong Delta

South
China Sea

Kampóng Chhnang
PHNOM PENH
Svay Riêng
Cân Tho

Stung Treng
Muang
Khổng
Phumi
Sámraóng
B A T D A M B A N G
C A M B O D I A

A M

Kâmpôt
Kampóng Saóm
Rach Gia

Malay
Peninsula

M A L A Y S I A

Songkhla
Pattani
Yala

Ko Phangan
Ko Samui
Nakhon Si
Thammarat
Trang
Hat Yai
Ko Phuket
Phuket

Ayutthaya
Ratchasima
BANGKOK
Chon Buri
Pattaya
Ko Chang
Gulf
of
Thailand

Thon Buri
Ratchaburi

Chumphon

Suratthani

Strait of Malacca

I N D O N E S I A

Sumatra

Tavoy

Mergui

Mergui
Archipelago

Isthmus of
Kra

Srinagarind
Res.

A n d a m a n   S e a

Andaman
Islands
(India)

Nicobar Islands
(India)

I N D I A N

O C E A N

119

MARITIME SOUTHEAST ASIA

BURMA

Andaman Sea

THAILAND

LAOS

VIETNAM

Gulf of Tongking

Hainan Dao

CAMBODIA

Gulf of Thailand

South Chi Sea

Spratly Is. (Disputed)

Nicobar Is. (India)

Banda Aceh

George Town ○ Kota Bharu
P. Pinang ○ Kuala Terengganu
Taiping ○
Ipoh ○ ○ Kuantan
Medan ○
Pematangsiantar ○ Kelang ○ ★ KUALA LUMPUR
Danau Toba Seremban ○
Melaka ○ ○ Johor Bharau
★ SINGAPORE

Kota Kinabalu
BANDAR SERI BEGAWAN
BRUNEI ★

Balabac

MALAYSIA

Sumatra

Equator Kep. Banyak

Padang ○
Kep. Mentawai

Pakanbaru ○
Jambi ○
Kep. Lingga
○ Pontianak
Kuching ○
Sibu ○
Sarawak
Rajang
Borneo
Peg. Muller
Samarinda
Balikpapan
Kapuas

Peg. Barisan

Hari

P. Bangka
○ Pangkalpinang
P. Belitung

Barito
Banjarmasin ○

Bengkulu ○
Palembang ○

INDONESIA

Java Sea

Tanjungkarang ○

★ JAKARTA
Bogor ○ ○ Cirebon
Bandung ○ Semarang
Yogyakarta ○ Malang
Surabaya
Jember
Bali
Lor
Denp

Java

0°

10°

INDIAN OCEAN

Java Trench

0 km   400
0 miles   400

THE PACIFIC OCEAN

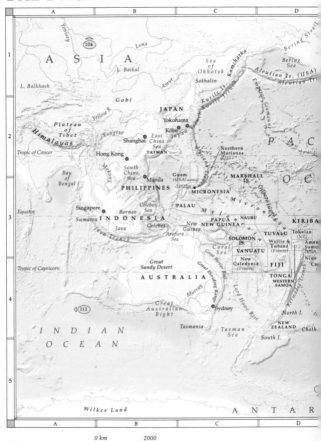

0 km   2000

0 miles   2000

AUSTRALASIA & OCEANIA

Borneo
Celebes
Sea
PALAU
MICRONESI
Equator
A S I A
M e
l a
n e
1
Java Sea
Celebes
Banda
Sea
PAPUA
NEW GUINEA
Bismarck
Archipelago
New Britain
Irian Jaya
New Guinea
Mt. Wilhelm
4509m
Java
Java Trench
Flores
Arafura
Sea
Solomon
Sea
SOLON
Sumba
Timor
Bathurst I.
Melville I.
Torres Strait
Timor
Sea
Coral Sea Islands
(Australia)
North
Australian
Basin
C. Londonderry
Arnhem
Land
Gulf of
Carpentaria
Cape
York
Peninsula
C o r a l
S e a
2
Victoria
Fitzroy
Great Barrier Reef
Cape
Tropic of Capricorn
Great
Sandy Desert
L. Disappointment
L. Mackay
Macdonnell
Ranges
Great Dividing Range
Fraser I.
Dirk Hartog I.
Gibson Desert
L. Carnegie
Uluru 868m
(Ayer's Rock)
A U S T R A L I A
Perth Basin
Great Victoria Desert
L. Barlee
Lake Eyre
-16m
3
Nullarbor Plain
L. Torrens
Flinders Range
Darling
C. Leeuwin
L. Gairdner
Murray
Great Australian
Bight
Mt. Kosciusko
2228m
Kangaroo I.
Cape Howe
4
Bass Strait
King I.
Tas m
Flinders I.
Sea
112
Tasmania
I N D I A N
South East Cape
Tasman
Plateau
O C E A N
South Australian Basin
5

0 km 1000

0 miles 1000

MARSHALL IS.

Kingman Reef *(USA)*
Palmyra Atoll *(USA)*

Baker & Howland Is. *(USA)*

Jarvis Island *(USA)*

Equator

PACIFIC

OCEAN

Gilbert Is.

Line Islands

KIRIBATI

Phoenix Is.

Polynesia

TUVALU

Tokelau
(New Zealand)

Northern
Cook Is.

Marquesas Is.

WESTERN
SAMOA

Wallis & Futuna
(France)

American
Samoa
(USA)

Cook Islands
(New Zealand)

French Polynesia
(France)

Vanua Levu

Niue
(New Zealand)

Tahiti

Viti Levu

TONGA

Iles Loyauté

FIJI

Southern Cook Is.

Society Islands

Tropic of Capricorn

South Fiji
Basin

Norfolk I.
(Australia)

Kermadec
Islands
(NZ)

North Cape

Kermadec Trench

Bay
of
Plenty

East Cape

PACIFIC

North I.

OCEAN

South I.

NEW
ZEALAND

Cook Strait

Cook ▲
764m.

Canterbury Bight

Chatham I.
(NZ)

Foveaux Strait

Stewart I.

Southwest Pacific Basin

Auckland I.
(NZ)

125

THE SOUTHWEST PACIFIC

0 km   400

0 miles   400

WESTERN AUSTRALIA

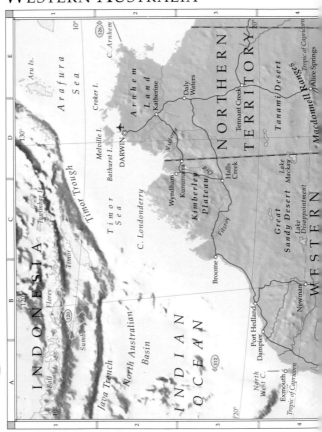

0 km · 400

0 miles · 400

SOUTHEAST AUSTRALIA

0 km   400

0 miles   400

NEW ZEALAND

0 km   200
0 miles   200

ATLANTIC OCEAN

Scotia Ridge

Falkland Is. (UK)

Brazilian zone of interest

ATLANTIC

Queen

South Shetland Is. (UK)

South Orkney Is. (UK)

British Antarctic Territory (UK)

Weddell Sea

Ritser-Larsen Ice Shelf

Cape Horn

Antarctic Peninsula

Chilean Claim

Argentina Claim

ANTA

Bellingshausen Sea

Alexander I.

Ronne Ice Shelf

Berkner I.

South Pole Plateau

Graham Land

Antarctic Circle

Vinson Massif 5140m

Ellsworth Land

Transantarctic Mountains

So

P

Pine Island Bay

Marie Byrd Land

Mount Kirkpatrick 4528m Mt. Markh 435.

Amundsen Sea

Lesser Antarctica

Mt. Sidley 4181m

Ross Ice Shelf

Peter the First I. (Norway)

Average extent of winter sea ice

Cape Colbeck

Limit of permanent pack

PACIFIC

OCEAN

Southeast Pacific Basin

Ross Sea

Ross Dependenc

0 km 750

0 miles 750

OCEAN

Limit of permanent pack ice

aud Land (Norway)

Lutzow-Holm Bay

Enderby Land

Average extent of winter sea ice

R C T I C A

Australian Antarctic Territory

Cape Darnley

Lambert Glacier

Mackenzie Bay

Prydz Bay

Princess Elizabeth Land

Antarctic Circle

Greater Antarctica

Kerguelen Plateau

Shackleton Ice Shelf

Davis Sea

Cape Poinsett

INDIAN

OCEAN

34

stralian Antarctic Territory

Terre Adélie (France)

Mt. Erebus 3794m

ardo nd

Mt. Shafer 3600m

Victoria Land

Wilkes Land

Southwest Pacific Basin

NZ)

Balleny Is.

GLOSSARY OF ABBREVIATIONS

This glossary provides a comprehensive guide to the abbreviations used in this Atlas.

abbrev. abbreviation
Afgh. Afghanistan
Amh. Amharic
anc. ancient
Ar. Arabic
Arm. Armenia/Armenian
Aus. Austria
Aust. Australia
Az. Azerbaijan/Azerbaijani

Bas. Basque
Bel. Belorussian
Belg. Belgium
Bos. & Herz. Bosnia & Herzegovina
Bul. Bulgarian
Bulg. Bulgaria
Bur. Burmese

C Central
C. Cape
Cam. Cambodian
Cast. Castilian
Chin. Chinese
Cord. Cordillera (Spanish for mountain range)
Cz. Czech
Czech Rep. Czech Republic

D.C. District of Columbia
Dan. Danish
Dominican Rep. Dominican Republic

E East
Emb. Embalse
Eng. English
Est. Estonia/Estonian

Faer. Faeroese
Fin. Finnish
Flem. Flemish
Fr. France/French

Geo. Georgia
Geor. Georgian
Ger. Germany/German
Gk. Greek

Heb. Hebrew
Hung. Hungary/Hungarian

I. Island
Ind. Indonesian
Is. Islands
It. Italian

Kaz. Kazakh
Kep. Kepulauan (Indonesian/Malay for island group)
Kir. Kirghiz
Kor. Korean
Kurd. Kurdish
Kyrgy. Kyrgyzstan

L. Lake, Lago
Lat. Latvia
Latv. Latvian
Leb. Lebanon
Liech. Liechtenstein
Lith. Lithuania/Lithuanian
Lux. Luxembourg

m metres
Mac. Macedonia
Med. Sea Mediterranean Sea
Mold. Moldavia
Mt. Mount/Mountain
Mts. Mountains

N North
N. Korea North Korea
Neth. Netherlands
NW Northwest
NZ New Zealand

P. Pulau (Indonesian/Malay for island)
Peg. Pegunungan (Indonesian/Malay for mountain range)
Per. Persian
Pol. Poland/Polish
Port. Portuguese
prev. previously

R. River, Rio, Río
Res. Reservoir
Rom. Romania/Romanian
Rus. Russian
Russ. Fed. Russian Federation

S South
S. Korea South Korea
SA South Africa
SCr. Serbo-Croatian
Slvka. Slovakia
Slvna. Slovenia
Som. Somali
Sp. Spanish

St, St. Saint
Str. Strait
Swed. Swedish
Switz. Switzerland

Tajik. Tajikistan
Th. Thai
Turk. Turkish
Turkm. Turkmen
Turkmen. Turkmenistan

U.A.E. United Arab Emirates
UK United Kingdom
Ukr. Ukrainian
USA United States of America
Uzb. Uzbek
Uzbek. Uzbekistan

var. variant
Vdkhr. Vodokhranilishche (Russian for reservoir)
Vdskh. Vodoskhovyshche (Ukrainian for reservoir)
Ven. Venezuela

W West
W. Sahara Western Sahara
Wel. Welsh

Yugo. Yugoslavia

Dorling Kindersley Cartography would like to thank the following for their assistance in producing this Atlas:

James Anderson, Laura Porter, Margaret Hynes, Ruth Duxbury, Roger Bullen, Julie Phillis, Robin Giddings and Tony Chambers.

INDEX

A

Albury Australia 130 B3
Alcácer do Sal Portugal 72 C4
Alcalá de Henares Spain 73 E3
Alchevs'k Ukraine 89 G3
Aldabra Group *Island group* Seychelles 59 G1
Aleg Mauritania 52 C3
Aleksandriya *see* Oleksandriya
Aleksandropol' *see* Gyumri
Aleksinac Yugoslavia 80 E4
Alençon France 70 B3
Alessandria Italy 76 A2
Ålesund Norway 65 A5
Aleutian Islands *Islands* Alaska, USA 16 A3
Aleutian Trench *Undersea feature* Pacific Ocean 122 D1
Alexander Island *Island* Antarctica 132 B2
Alexandretta *see* İskenderun
Alexandria Egypt 54 B1
Alexandria Louisiana, USA 28 B3
Alexandroúpoli Greece 84 D3
Al Fāshir *see* El Fasher
Alföld *Plain* Hungary 79 D7
Algarve *Region* Portugal 72 C4
Algeciras Spain 72 D5
Algeria *Country* N Africa 50-51
Alghero Italy 77 A5
Algiers *Capital of* Algeria 50 D1
Al Ḥasakah Syria 98 D2
Al Ḥillah Iraq *var.* Hilla 100 B3
Al Ḥudaydah Yemen 101 B7
Al Hufūf Saudi Arabia 101 C5
Alicante Spain 73 F4
Alice Springs Australia 126 A5 128 E4
Al Jawf Saudi Arabia 100 B4
Al Jazīrah *Region* Iraq/Syria 98 E2
Al Jīzah *see* El Gîza
Al Karak Jordan 99 B6
Al Khārijah *see* El Khârga
Al Khums Libya 51 F2
Al Khurtūm *see* Khartoum
Alkmaar Netherlands 66 C2
Al Kufrah Libya 51 H4
Al Lādhiqīyah Syria *Eng.* Latakia 88 B3
Allahābād India 114 C4
Allenstein *see* Olsztyn

Allentown Pennsylvania, USA 21 F4
Alma-Ata *Capital of* Kazakhstan *Rus./Kaz.* Almaty 95 C5
Al Madīnah Saudi Arabia *Eng.* Medina 100 A5
Al Mafraq Jordan 99 B5
Almalyk Uzbekistan *Uzb.* Olmaliq 103 E2
Al Manāmah *see* Manama
Al Marj Libya 51 G2
Almaty *see* Alma-Ata
Al Mawşil Iraq *Eng.* Mosul 100 B3
Almelo Netherlands 66 E3
Almería Spain 73 E5
Al Mukallā Yemen 101 C7
Alofi *Capital of* Niue 127 F5
Alor, Kepulauan *Island group* Indonesia 121 E5
Alps *Mountain range* C Europe 60 D4
Al Qāhirah *see* Cairo
Al Qāmishlī Syria *var.* Kamishli 98 E1
Al Qunayţirah Syria 98 B4
Altai Mountains *Mountain Range* C Asia 106 C2
Altamura Italy 77 E5
Altay China 106 C2
Altay Mongolia 106 D2
Altun Shan *Mountain Range* China 106 B4
Alturas California, USA 24 B4
Al Wajh Saudi Arabia 100 A5
Alytus Lithuania *Pol.* Olita 87 B5
Amakusa-shotō *Island group* Japan 111 A6
Amami-Ō-shima *Island* Japan 111 A8
Amara *see* Al 'Amārah
Amarillo Texas, USA 27 E2
Amazon *River* South America 36 C2
Amazon Delta *Wetland* Brazil 36 D2
Amazonia *Region* C South America 40 C2
Ambanja Madagascar 59 G2
Ambarchik Russian Federation 95 G2
Ambato Ecuador 38 A4

Amboasary Madagascar 59 F4
Ambon Indonesia 121 F4
Ambositra Madagascar 59 G3
Ambriz Angola 58 B1
Ameland *Island* Netherlands 66 D1
American Falls Reservoir *Reservoir* Idaho, USA 24 E4
American Samoa *External territory* USA, Pacific Ocean 122 D3
Amersfoort Netherlands 66 D3
Amiens France 70 C3
Amīndīvi Islands *Island group* India 116 C2
Amirante Islands *Island group* Seychelles 59 H1
Amman *Capital of* Jordan 99 B5
Ammassalik Greenland *var.* Angmagssalik 62 C4
Ammochostos *see* Gazimağusa
Āmol Iran 100 C3
Amorgós *Island* Greece 85 D6
Amritsar India 114 D2
Amsterdam *Capital of* Netherlands 66 C3
Amstetten Austria 75 D6
Am Timan Chad 56 C3
Amu Darya *River* C Asia 102 D3
Amundsen Gulf *Sea feature* Canada 17 F2
Amundsen Sea Antarctica 132 B4
Amur *River* E Asia 93 F3 105 E1
Anadolu Dağları *see* Doğu Karadeniz Dağları
Anadyr' Russian Federation 95 H1
Anápolis Brazil 41 F4
Anatolia *Region* SE Europe 83 G3
Anchorage Alaska, USA 16 C3
Ancona Italy 76 C3
Andalucía *Region* Spain 72 D4
Andaman Islands *Island group* India 117 H2 119 A5
Andaman Sea Indian Ocean 112 D3
Andaman-Nicobar Ridge *Undersea feature* Indian Ocean 117 H3
Andes *Mountain range* South America 37 B6

Andijon *see* Andizhan

Andizhan Uzbekistan *Uzb.* Andijon 103 F2

Andorra *Country* SW Europe 71 B6

Andorra la Vella *Capital of* Andorra 71 B6

Ándros Greece 85 C5

Andros Island *Island* Bahamas 34 C1

Angara *River* C Asia 93 E2

Angara Basin *see* Fram Basin

Ángel de la Guarda, Isla *Island* Mexico 30 B2

Angel Falls *Waterfall* Venezuela 36 C2

Angeles Philippines 121 E1

Ångermanälven *River* Sweden 64 C4

Angers France 70 B4

Anglesey *Island* Wales, UK 69 C5

Angmagssalik *see* Ammassalik

Angola *Country* C Africa 58

Angola Basin *Undersea feature* Atlantic Ocean 47 D5

Angora *see* Ankara

Angoulême France 71 B5

Angren Uzbekistan 103 E2

Anguilla *External territory* UK, West Indies 35

Anjouan *Island* Comoros 59 G2

Ankara *Capital of* Turkey *prev.* Angora 96 C3

Annaba Algeria 51 E1

An Nafūd *Desert region* Saudi Arabia 100 B4

An Najaf Iraq *var.* Najaf 100 B4

Annapolis Maryland, USA 21 F4

Ann Arbor Michigan, USA 20 C3

An Nāşirīyah Iraq *var.* Nasiriya 100 C4

Annecy France 71 D5

Anshan China 108 D4

Antakya Turkey *var.* Hatay 96 D4

Antaïaha Madagascar 59 G2

Antalya Turkey *prev.* Adalia 96 B4

Antalya, Gulf of *see* Antalya Körfezi

Antalya Körfezi *Sea feature* Mediterranean Sea *Eng.* Gulf of Antalya, *var.* Gulf of Adalia 96 B4

Antananarivo *Capital of* Madagascar *prev.* Tananarive 59 G3

Antarctica 132-133

Antarctic Peninsula *Peninsula* Antarctica 132 A2

Antequera Spain 72 D5

Anticosti, Île d' *Island* Canada 19 E3

Antigua *Island* Antigua & Barbuda 35

Antigua & Barbuda *Country* West Indies 35

Anti-Lebanon *Mountains* Lebanon/Syria 98 B4

Antofagasta Chile 44 B2

Antsirañana Madagascar 59 G2

Antsohihy Madagascar 59 G2

Antwerp *see* Antwerpen

Antwerpen Belgium *Eng.* Antwerp 67 C5

Aoga-shima *Island* Japan 111 D6

Aomori Japan 110 D3

Aorangi *see* Cook, Mount

Aosta Italy 76 A2

Apeldoorn Netherlands 66 D3

Apennines *see* Appennino

Apia *Capital of* Western Samoa 127 F4

Appalachian Mountains *Mountain range* E USA 15 F4

Appennino *Mountain range* Italy *Eng.* Apennines 60 D5 76 C4

Apure *River* Venezuela 36 B2

Aputiteeq Greenland 62 D3

Aqaba *see* Al 'Aqabah

Aqaba, Gulf of *Sea feature* Red Sea *Ar.* Khalīj al 'Aqabah 99 A8

'Aqabah, Khalīj al *see* Red Sea

Âqcheh Afghanistan *var.* Aqcheh 102 D3

Aqcheh *see* Âqcheh

Arabian Basin *Undersea feature* Indian Ocean 116 B2

Arabian Peninsula *Peninsula* Asia 83 H5 92 B5

Arabian Sea Indian Ocean 112 B3

Aracaju Brazil 41 H3

Arad Romania 88 A4

Arafura Sea Asia/Australasia 122 B3

Araguaia *River* Brazil 41 E3

Arāk Iran 100 C3

Araks *see* Aras

Arak's *see* Aras

Aral Sea *Inland sea* Kazakhstan/Uzbekistan 92 C3

Ararat, Mount *Peak* Turkey *var.* Great Ararat, *Turk.* Büyükağrı Dağı 92 B4

Aras *River* SW Asia *Arm.* Arak's, *Per.* Rūd-e Aras, *Rus.* Araks, *Turk.* Aras Nehri 97 G3

Aras Nehri *see* Aras

Arauca Colombia 38 C2

Arauca *River* Colombia/Venezuela 38 C2

Arbatax Italy 77 A5

Arbīl Iraq *Kurd.* Hawlêr 100 B3

Arctic Ocean 16-17

Arda *River* Bulgaria/Greece 84 C3

Ardennes *Region* W Europe 67 D7

Arendal Norway 65 A6

Arensburg *see* Kuressaare

Arequipa Peru 40 B4

Arezzo Italy 76 C3

Argentina *Country* S South America 44-45

Argentine Basin *Undersea feature* Atlantic Ocean 47 B6

Argentine claim in Antarctica 132 C2

Argentino, Lago *Lake* Argentina 45 B7

Århus Denmark 65 A7

Arica Chile 44 B1

Arizona *State* USA 26 B2

Arkansas *State* USA 28 B1

Arkansas *River* C USA 15 E4

Arkhangel'sk Russian Federation 90 C3 94 C2

Arles France 71 D6

Arlon Belgium 67 D8

Armenia *Country* SW Asia 97 G2

Armenia Colombia 38 B3

Armidale Australia 130 C2

Arnhem Netherlands 66 D4

Arnhem, Cape *Coastal feature* Australia 128 E2

B

Bābol Iran 100 D3

Babruysk Belorussia *Rus.* Bobruysk 87 D6

Bacan, Pulau *Island* Indonesia 121 F4

Bačka Topola Yugoslavia 80 D2

Bacolod Philippines 121 E2

Bacău Romania 88 C4

Badain Jaran Shamo *Desert region* China 107 E3

Badajoz Spain 72 C4

Badalona Spain 73 G2

Baden Switzerland 75 E6

Bādiyat ash Shām *see* Syrian Desert

Bafatá Guinea-Bissau 52 C4

Baffin Bay *Sea feature* Atlantic Ocean 46 B1

Baffin Island *Island* Canada 15 F1

Bafoussam Cameroon 56 B4

Bagdad *see* Baghdad

Bagé Brazil 42 C4

Baghdad *Capital of* Iraq *var.* Bagdad, *Ar.* Baghdād 100 B3

Baghdād *see* Baghdad

Baghlān Afghanistan 103 E4

Baguio Philippines 121 E1

Bahamas *Country* West Indies, Atlantic Ocean 34

Baharden *see* Bakherden

Bahāwalpur Pakistan 114 C3

Bäherden *see* Bakherden

Bahía, Islas de la *Islands* Honduras 32 D2

Bahir Dar Ethiopia 54 C4

Bahrain *Country* SW Asia 101 C5

Baia Mare Romania 88 B3

Bai'an China 108 D2

Baikal, Lake *see* Baykal, Ozero

Bairiki *Capital of* Kiribati 127 E2

Baja Hungary 79 C7

Baja California *Peninsula* Mexico *Eng.* Lower California 30 B2

Bajo Nuevo *Island* Colombia 33 F2

Baker Oregon, USA 24 C3

Baker & Howell Islands *External territory* USA, Pacific Ocean 127 F2

Bakersfield California, USA 25 C7

Bakharden *see* Bakherden

Bakherden Turkmenistan *prev.* Bakharden, *var.* Baharden, *Turkm.* Bäherden 102 B3

Bākhtarān Iran *prev.* Kermānshāh 100 C3

Bakı *see* Baku

Baku *Capital of* Azerbaijan *Az.* Bakı, *var.* Baky 96 A3

Baky *see* Baku

Balabac Strait *Sea feature* South China Sea/Sulu Sea 120 D2

Ba'labakk *see* Baalbek

Balakovo Russian Federation 91 C6

Bālā Morghāb Afghanistan 102 D4

Balaton *Lake* Hungary *var.* Lake Balaton, *Ger.* Plattensee 79 C7

Balaton, Lake *see* Balaton

Balbina, Represa *Reservoir* Brazil 40 D2

Baleares, Islas *Island group* Spain *Eng.* Balearic Islands 73 H3 82 C3

Balearic Islands *see* Baleares, Islas

Bali *Island* Indonesia 120 D5

Balıkesir Turkey 96 A3

Balikpapan Indonesia 120 D4

Balkan Mountains *Mountain range* Bulgaria *Bul.* Stara Planina 84 C2

Balkhash Kazakhstan 94 C5

Balkhash, Lake *see* Balkhash, Ozero

Balkhash, Ozero *Lake* Kazakhstan *Eng.* Lake Balkhash 92 C3 94 C5

Ballarat Australia 130 B4

Balleny Islands *Island group* Antarctica 133 E5

Balsas *River* Mexico 31 E5

Bălţi Moldavia 88 D3

Baltic Port *see* Paldiski

Baltic Sea Atlantic Ocean 65 C7

Baltimore Maryland, USA 21 F4

Baltischport *see* Paldiski

Baltiski *see* Paldiski

Baltiysk Kaliningrad, Russian Federation *prev.* Pillau 86 A4

Bamako *Capital of* Mali 52 D4

Bambari Central African Republic 56 C4

Bamenda Cameroon 56 B4

Banaba Brazil Kiribati *prev.* Ocean Island 127 E2

Banda, Laut *see* Banda Sea

Banda Aceh Indonesia 120 A3

Banda Sea *Sea feature* Pacific Ocean *Ind.* Laut Banda 105 E5 121 F4

Bandar-e 'Abbās Iran 100 D4

Bandar-e Būshehr Iran 100 C4

Bandar Seri Begawan *Capital of* Brunei 120 D3

Bandon Oregon, USA 24 A3

Bandundu Zaire 57 C6

Bandung Indonesia 120 C5

Bangalore India 116 D2

Banggai, Kepulauan *Island group* Indonesia 121 E4

Banghāzī Libya *Eng.* Benghazi 51 G2

Bangka, Pulau *Island* Indonesia 120 C4

Bangkok *Capital of* Thailand *Th.* Krung Thep 119 C5

Bangladesh *Country* S Asia 115

Bangor Northern Ireland, UK 69 B5

Bangor Maine, USA 21 G2

Bangui *Capital of* Central African Republic 57 C5

Bani *River* Mali 52 D3

Banī Suwayf *see* Beni Suef

Banja Luka Bosnia & Herzegovina 80 B3

Banjarmasin Indonesia 120 D4

Banjul *Capital of* Gambia 52 B3

Banks Island *Island* Canada 17 E2

Banks Island *Island* Vanuatu, Pacific Ocean 126 D4

Banská Bystrica Slovakia *Ger.* Neusohl, *Hung.* Besztercebánya 79 C6

Bantry Bay *Sea feature* Ireland 69 A6

Banyak, Kepulauan *Island group* Indonesia 120 A3

Banyo Cameroon 56 B4

Baoji China 109 B5

Baotou China 107 E3

Ba'qūbah C Iraq 100 B3

Baracaldo Spain 73 E1

Baranavichy Belorussia *Rus.* Baranovichi, *Pol.* Baranowicze 87 C6

Baranovichi *see* Baranavichy

Baranowicze *see* Baranavichy

Barbados *Country* West Indies 35 E4

Barbuda *Island* Antigua & Barbuda 35 G3

Barcelona Spain 73 G2

Barcelona Venezuela 39 E1

Bareilly India 115 E3

Barentsburg Svalbard 63 G2

Barents Sea Arctic Ocean 64 E1

Bari Italy 77 E5

Barinas Venezuela 38 D2

Barisan, Pegunungan *Mountains* Indonesia 120 B4

Bar-le-Duc France 70 D3

Barito *River* Indonesia 120 D4

Barlee, Lake *Lake* Australia 124 B3 129 B 5

Barnaul Russian Federation 94 D4

Barnstaple England, UK 69 C7

Barquisimeto Venezuela 38 D1

Barra *Island* Scotland, UK 68 B3

Barranquilla Colombia 38 B1

Barrow *River* Ireland 69 B6

Barstow California, USA 25 C7

Bartang *River* Tajikistan 103 F3

Bartica Guyana 39 G2

Barysaw Belorussia *Rus.* Borisov 87 D5

Basarabeasca Moldavia 88 D4

Basel Switzerland 75 A7

Basque Provinces *Region* Spain *Sp.* País Vasco 73 E1

Basra *see* Al Başrah

Bassein Burma 118 A4

Basse-Terre *Capital of* Guadeloupe 35 G4

Basseterre *Capital of* St Kitts & Nevis 35 G3

Bass Strait *Sea feature* Australia 130 B4

Bastia Corse, France 71 E7

Bastogne Belgium 67 D7

Bata Equatorial Guinea 56 A5

Batangas Philippines 121 E1

Bătdâmbâng Cambodia 119 D5

Bath England, UK 69 D7

Bathurst Australia 130 C3

Bathurst Canada 19 F4

Bathurst Island *Island* Australia 128 D2

Bathurst Island *Island* Canada 17 F2

Batman Turkey *var.* İluh 97 F2

Batna Algeria 51 E1

Baton Rouge Louisiana, USA 28 B3

Batticaloa Sri Lanka 117 E3

Bat'umi Georgia 97 F2

Bauchi Nigeria 53 G4

Bauru Brazil 42 D2

Bavarian Alps *Mountains* Austria/Germany 75 C7

Bayamo Cuba 34 C2

Bay City Michigan, USA 20 C3

Baydhabo Somalia 55 D6

Baykal, Ozero *Lake* Russian Federation *Eng.* Lake Baikal 93 E3 95 F4

Bayonne France 71 A6

Bayramaly Turkmenistan 102 C3

Bayrūt *see* Beirut

Beaufort Sea Arctic Ocean 17 E2

Beaufort West South Africa 58 C5

Beaumont Texas, USA 27 H4

Beauvais France 70 C3

Béchar Algeria 50 C2

Be'ér Sheva' Israel 99 A6

Beijing *Capital of* China *var.* Peking 108 C4

Beira Mozambique 59 E3

Beirut *Capital of* Lebanon *var.* Beyrouth, Bayrūt 98 B4

Beja Portugal 72 C4

Béjaïa Algeria 51 E1

Bek-Budi *see* Karshi

Békéscsaba Hungary 79 D7

Belarus *see* Belorussia

Belau see Palau

Belcher Islands *Islands* Canada 18 C2

Beledweyne Somalia 55 D5

Belém Brazil 41 F2

Belfast Northern Ireland, UK 69 B5

Belfort France 70 E4

Belgaum India 116 C1

Belgium *Country* W Europe 67

Belgorod Russian Federation 91 A5

Belgrade *Capital of* Yugoslavia *SCr.* Beograd 80 D3

Belitung, Pulau *Island* Indonesia 120 C4

Belize *Country* Central America 32

Belize City Belize 32 C1

Bella Unión Uruguay 42 B4

Belle Île *Island* France 70 A4

Belle Isle, Strait of *Sea feature* Canada 15 G3 19 H3

Bellevue Washington, USA 24 B2*

Bellingham Washington, USA 24 B1

Bellingshausen Sea Antarctica 47 A8 132 A3

Bello Colombia 38 B2

Belluno Italy 76 C2

Bellville South Africa 58 C5

Belmopan *Capital of* Belize 32 C1

Belo Horizonte Brazil 41 G5 43 F1

Belorussia *Country* E Europe *var.* Belarus 87

Belostok *see* Białystok

Beloye More Arctic Ocean *Eng.* White Sea 61 F1 90 C3

Bend Oregon, USA 24 B3

Bendery *see* Tighina

Bendigo Australia 130 B4

Benevento Italy 77 D5

Bengal, Bay of *Sea feature* Indian Ocean 112 C3

Benghazi *see* Banghāzī

Bengkulu Indonesia 120 B4

Benguela Angola 58 B2

Beni *River* Bolivia 40 C4

Benidorm Spain 73 F4

Beni Mellal Morocco 50 C2

Benin *Country* N Africa *prev.* Dahomey 53

Benin, Bight of *Sea feature* W Africa 53 F5

Benin City Nigeria 53 F5

Beni Suef Egypt *var.* Banī Suwayf 54 B1

Benue *River* Cameroon/Nigeria 53 G4

Beograd *see* Belgrade

Berat Albania 81 B3

Berbera Somalia 54 D4

Berbérati Central African Republic 56 C5

Berdyans'k Ukraine 88 G4

Berezina see Byerazina

Bergamo Italy 76 B2

Bergen Norway 65 A5

Bering Sea Pacific Ocean 122 D1

Bering Strait Sea feature Bering Sea/Chukchi Sea 122 D1

Berkner Island Island Antarctica 132 C2

Berlin Capital of Germany 74 D3

Bermejo River Argentina 44 D2

Bermuda External territory UK, Atlantic Ocean 46 B3

Bern Capital of Switzerland Fr. Berne 75 A7

Berne see Bern

Bertoua Cameroon 57 B5

Besançon France 70 D4

Besztercebánya see Banská Bystrica

Bethlehem West Bank 99 B5

Beuthen see Bytom

Beyrouth see Beirut

Béziers France 71 C6

Bezmein see Byuzmeyin

Bhamo Burma 118 B2

Bhātāpāra India 114 C4

Bhāvnagar India 114 C4

Bhōpal India 114 D4

Bhutan Country S Asia 115

Biak, Pulau Island Indonesia 121 G4

Białystok Poland Rus. Belostok 78 E3

Biel Switzerland 75 A7

Bielitz-Biala see Bielsko-Biała

Bielsko-Biała Poland Ger. Bielitz-Biala 79 C5

Bighorn Mountains Mountains C USA 22 C2

Big Spring Texas, USA 27 E3

Bihać Bosnia & Herzegovina 80 B3

Bihār State India 115 F3

Bijelo Polje Yugoslavia 80 D4

Bīkaner India 114 C3

Bila Tserkva Ukraine 89 E2

Bilbao Spain 73 E1

Billings Montana, USA 22 C2

Biloxi Mississippi, USA 28 C3

Biltine Chad 56 D3

Binghamton New York, USA 21 F3

Bío Bío River Chile 45 B5

Birāk Libya 51 F3

Biratnagar Nepal 115 F3

Birganj Nepal 115 F3

Birmingham England, UK 69 D6

Birmingham Alabama, USA 28 D2

Birni-Nkonni Niger 53 F3

Birsen see Biržai

Biržai Lithuania Ger. Birsen 86 C4

Biscay, Bay of Sea feature Atlantic Ocean 71 A5 73 E1

Biscay Plain Undersea feature Atlantic Ocean 60 B4

Bishkek Capital of Kyrgyzstan prev. Frunze, Pishpek 103 F2

Bishop California, USA 25 C6

Biskra Algeria 51 E2

Bismarck North Dakota, USA 23 E2

Bismarck Archipelago Island group Papua New Guinea 126 B3

Bissau Capital of Guinea-Bissau 52 B4

Bitola Macedonia 81 D6

Bitterroot Range Mountains NW USA 24 D2

Biwa-ko Lake Japan 111 C5

Bizerte Tunisia 51 E1

Bjelovar Croatia 80 B2

Black Drin River Albania/Macedonia 81 D5

Black Forest see Schwarzwald

Black Hills Mountains C USA 22 D3

Blackpool England, UK 69 C5

Black River River China/Vietnam 118 D3

Black Sea Asia/Europe 61 F1 82 A4

Black Volta River Ghana/Ivory Coast 53 E4

Blackwater River Ireland 69 A6

Blagoevgrad Bulgaria 84 B3

Blagoveshchensk Russian Federation 95 G4

Blanca, Bahía Sea feature Argentina 37 C6

Blantyre Malawi 59 E2

Blenheim New Zealand 131 G3

Blida Algeria 50 D1

Bloemfontein South Africa 58 D4

Blois France 70 C4

Bloomington Indiana, USA 20 C4

Bluefields Nicaragua 33 E3

Blue Mountains Mountains W USA 24 C3

Blue Nile River Ethiopia/Sudan 55 C4

Blumenau Brazil 42 D3

Bo Sierra Leone 52 C4

Boa Vista Brazil 40 D1

Bobo-Dioulasso Burkina 53 E4

Bobruysk see Babruysk

Boca de la Serpiente see Serpent's Mouth, The

Bochum Germany 74 A4

Bodø Norway 64 C3

Bodrum Turkey 96 A4

Bogor Indonesia 120 C5

Bogotá Capital of Colombia 38 B3

Bo Hai Sea feature Yellow Sea 108 D4

Bohemian Forest Region Czech Rep 75 D6

Bohol Island Philippines 121 E2

Boise Idaho, USA 24 D3

Bokhara see Bukhara

Bol Chad 56 B3

Bolivia Country C South America 40-41

Bologna Italy 76 C3

Bolton England, UK 69 D5

Bolzano Italy Ger. Bozen 76 C1

Boma Zaire 57 B7

Bombay India var. Mumbai 115 C5 116 C1

Bomu River Central African Republic/Zaire 57 D5

Bonete, Cerro Peak Chile 37 B5

Bongo, Massif des Upland Central African Republic 56 D4

Bongor Chad 56 B3

Bonn Germany 75 A5

Boosaaso Somalia 54 E4

Borås Sweden 65 B7

Bordeaux France 71 B5

Borger Texas, USA 27 E2

Borisov *see* Barysaw

Borlänge Sweden 65 C6

Borneo *Island* SE Asia 120-121

Bornholm *Island* Denmark 65 C8

Bosanski Šamac Bosnia & Herzegovina 80 C3

Bosna *River* Bosnia & Herzegovina 80 B3

Bosnia & Herzegovina *Country* SE Europe 80-81

Bosporus *Sea feature* Turkey *Turk.* İstanbul Boğazi 96 B2

Bossangoa Central African Republic 56 C4

Boston Massachusetts, USA 21 G3

Botevgrad Bulgaria 84 C2

Bothnia, Gulf of *Sea feature* Baltic Sea 65 C5

Botoşani Romania 88 C3

Botswana *Country* southern Africa 58

Bouaké Ivory Coast 52 D4

Bouar Central African Republic 56 C4

Bougainville Island *Island* Papua New Guinea 126 C3

Bougouni Mali 52 D4

Boulder Colorado, USA 22 C4

Boulogne-sur-Mer France 70 C2

Bourges France 70 C4

Bourgogne *Region* France *Eng.* Burgundy 70 D4

Bourke Australia 130 B2

Bournemouth England, UK 69 D7

Bouvet Island *External territory* Norway, Atlantic Ocean 47 D7

Bowling Green Kentucky, USA 20 C5

Bozeman Montana, USA 22 B2

Bozen *see* Bolzano

Brač *Island* Croatia 80 B4

Bradford England, UK 69 D5

Braga Portugal 72 C2

Bragança Portugal 72 C2

Brahmaputra *River* S Asia 106 B5 115 G3

Brăila Romania 88 D4

Brainerd Minnesota, USA 23 F2

Brandon Canada 17 G5

Brasília *Capital of* Brazil 41 F4

Braşov Romania 88 C4

Bratislava *Capital of* Slovakia *Ger.* Pressburg, *Hung.* Pozsony 79 C6

Bratsk Russian Federation 95 E4

Braunau am Inn Austria 75 D6

Braunschweig Germany *Eng.* Brunswick 74 C4

Brazil *Country* South America 40-43

Brazil Basin *Undersea feature* Atlantic Ocean 47 C5

Brazilian Highlands *Upland* Brazil 41 G4

Brazos *River* SW USA 27 G3

Brazzaville *Capital of* Congo 57 B6

Brecon Beacons *Hills* Wales, UK 69 E7

Breda Netherlands 66 D4

Bregenz Austria 75 B7

Bremen Germany 74 B3

Bremerhaven Germany 74 B3

Brescia Italy 76 B2

Breslau *see* Wrocław

Brest Belorussia *Pol.* Brześć nad Bugiem, *prev.* Brześć Litewski, *Rus.* Brest-Litovsk 87 B6

Brest France 70 A3

Brest-Litovsk *see* Brest

Bretagne *Region* France *Eng.* Brittany 70 A3

Breton Sound *Inlet* Louisiana, USA 28 C4

Brezhnev *see* Naberezhnyye Chelny

Bria Central African Republic 56 D4

Bridgetown *Capital of* Barbados 35 H5

Brig Switzerland 75 D5

Brighton England, UK 69 E7

Brindisi Italy 77 E5

Brisbane Australia 130 D2

Bristol England, UK 69 D7

British Antarctic Territory *Territory* Antarctica 132 B2

British Columbia *Province* Canada 16-17

British Indian Ocean Territory *External territory* UK, Indian Ocean 112 C4

British Isles *Islands* W Europe 68-69

British Virgin Islands *External territory* UK, West Indies 35

Brittany *see* Bretagne

Brno Czech Republic *Ger.* Brünn 79 B5

Broken Arrow Oklahoma, USA 27 G1

Broken Hill Australia 130 B3

Broken Ridge *Undersea feature* Indian Ocean 113 D5

Bromberg *see* Bydgoszcz

Brooks Range *Mountains* Alaska, USA 17 F2

Broome Australia 128 C3

Brownfield Texas, USA 27 E3

Brownsville Texas, USA 27 G5

Bruges *see* Brugge

Brugge Belgium *Fr.* Bruges 67 A5

Brunei *Country* E Asia 120 D3

Brünn *see* Brno

Brunswick Georgia, USA 29 E3

Brunswick *see* Braunschweig

Brusa *see* Bursa

Brussel *see* Brussels

Brussels *Capital of* Belgium *Fr.* Bruxelles, *Flem.* Brussel 67 C6

Brüx *see* Most

Bruxelles *see* Brussels

Bryan Texas, USA 27 G3

Bryansk Russian Federation 91 A5 94 A2

Brześć Litewski *see* Brest

Brześć nad Bugiem *see* Brest

Bucaramanga Colombia 38 C2

Buchanan Liberia 52 C5

Bucharest *Capital of* Romania 88 C5

Budapest *Capital of* Hungary 79 C6

Budweis *see* České Budějovice

Buenaventura Colombia 38 B3

Buenos Aires *Capital of* Argentina 44 D4

Buenos Aires, Lago *Lake* Argentina/Chile 45 B6

Buffalo New York, USA 21 E3

Bug *River* E Europe 78 E3 88 C1

Bujumbura *Capital of* Burundi *prev.* Usumbura 55 B7

Bukavu Zaire 57 E6

Bukhara Uzbekistan *var.* Bokhara, *Uzb.* Bokhoro 102 D2

Bukhoro *see* Bukhara

Bulawayo Zimbabwe 58 D3

Bulgaria *Country* E Europe 84

Bumba Zaire 57 D5

Bunbury Australia 129 B6

Bundaberg Australia 126 C5 130 C1

Bunia Zaire 57 E5

Buraydah Saudi Arabia 101 B5

Burė Ethiopia 54 C4

Burgas Bulgaria 84 E2

Burgos Spain 73 E2

Burgundy *see* Bourgogne

Burkina *Country* W Africa 53

Burlington Iowa, USA 23 G4

Burlington Vermont, USA 21 F2

Burma *Country* SE Asia *var.* Myanmar 118-119

Burnie Tasmania 130 B4

Burns Oregon, USA 24 C3

Bursa Turkey *prev.* Brusa 96 B3

Burtnieku Ezers *Lake* Latvia 86 C3

Buru *Island* Indonesia 121 F4

Burundi *Country* C Africa 55

Butembo Zaire 57 E5

Butte Montana, USA 22 B2

Butuan Philippines 121 F2

Buurhakaba Somalia 55 D6

Buyo Reservoir *Reservoir* Ivory Coast 52 D5

Büyükağrı Dağı *see* Ararat, Mount

Buzău Romania 88 C4

Bydgoszcz Poland *Ger.* Bromberg 78 C3

Byerazino *River* Belorussia *Rus.* Berezina 87 D6

Bykhaw Belorussia *Rus.* Bykhov 87 D6

Bykhov *see* Bykhaw

Bytom Poland *Ger.* Beuthen 79 C5

Byuzmeyin Turkmenistan *prev.* Bezmein 102 B3

Byzantium *see* İstanbul

C

Caaguazú Paraguay 42 C2

Cabanatuan Philippines 121 E1

Cabimas Venezuela 38 C1

Cabinda *Exclave* Angola 57 B7 58 B1

Cabot Strait *Sea feature* Atlantic Ocean 19 G4

Čačak Yugoslavia 80 D4

Cáceres Spain 72 D3

Cachoeiro de Itapemirim Brazil 43 F1

Cadiz Philippines 121 E2

Cádiz Spain 72 D5

Caen France 70 B3

Caernarfon Wales, UK 69 C5

Cagayan de Oro Philippines 121 F2

Cagliari Italy 77 A6

Cahors France 71 B5

Cairns Australia 126 B4

Cairo *Capital of* Egypt *Ar.* Al Qāhirah, *var.* El Qāhira 54 B1

Čakovec Croatia 80 B2

Calabar Nigeria 53 G5

Calabria *Region* Italy 77 D6

Calafate Argentina 45 B7

Calais France 70 C2

Calais Maine, USA 21 H1

Calama Chile 44 B2

Calbayog Philippines 121 F2

Calcutta India 115 F4

Caldas da Rainha Portugal 72 B3

Caldwell Idaho, USA 25 C3

Caleta Olivia Argentina 45 C6

Calgary Canada 17 E5

Cali Colombia 38 B3

Calicut India *var.* Kozhikode 116 D2

California *State* USA 24-25

California, Golfo de *Sea feature* Pacific Ocean *Eng.* California, Gulf of 30 B2 123 F2

Callao Peru 40 A4

Caltagirone Italy 77 D7

Caltanissetta Italy 77 C7

Camagüey Cuba 34 C2

Cambodia *Country* SE Asia *Cam.* Kampuchea 118-119

Cambridge England, UK 69 E6

Cameroon *Country* W Africa 56-57

Camiri Bolivia 40 D5

Campbell Plateau *Undersea feature* Pacific Ocean 131 H4

Campeche Mexico 31 H4

Campeche, Bahía de *Sea feature* Mexico *Eng.* Gulf of Campeche 31 G4

Campina Grande Brazil 41 H3

Campinas Brazil 41 F5 43 E2

Campo Grande Brazil 41 E5 42 C1

Campos Brazil 41 G5 43 F2

Canada *Country* North America 16-17 18-19

Canada Basin *Undersea feature* Arctic Ocean *var.* Laurentian Basin 12 B3

Canadian River *River* SW USA 27 E2

Çanakkale Turkey 96 A2

Çanakkale Boğazı *see* Dardanelles

Canarias, Islas *Islands* Spain *Eng.* Canary Islands 46 C4 50 A2

Canary Basin *Undersea feature* Atlantic Ocean 46 C4

Canary Islands *see* Canarias, Islas

Canaveral, Cape *Coastal feature* Florida, USA 29 F4

Canberra *Capital of* Australia 130 C3

Cancún Mexico 31 H3

Caniapiscau *River* Canada 19 E2

Caniapiscau, Réservoir *Reservoir* Canada 19 E3

Canik Dağları *Mountains* Turkey 96 D2

Çankırı Turkey 96 C2

Cannes France 71 D6

Canoas Brazil 42 D4

Canterbury England, UK 69 E7

Canterbury Bight *Sea feature* Pacific Ocean 131 G4

Canterbury Plains *Plain* New Zealand 131 G4

Cần Thơ Vietnam 119 D6

Canton Ohio, USA 20 D4

Canton *see* Guangzhou

Cape Basin *Undersea feature* Atlantic Ocean 49 C7 58 B5

Cape Coast Ghana 53 E5

Cape Town South Africa 58 C5

Cape Verde *Country* Atlantic Ocean 52 A3

Cape Verde Basin *Undersea feature* Atlantic Ocean 46 C4

Cape York Peninsula *Peninsula* Australia 124 C2

Cap-Haïtien Haiti 34 D3

Capri, Isola di *Island* Italy 77 C5

Caquetá *River* Colombia 38 C4

CAR *see* Central African Republic

Caracas *Capital of* Venezuela 38 D1

Carazinho Brazil 42 C3

Carbondale Illinois, USA 20 B5

Carcassonne France 71 C6

Cardiff Wales, UK 69 C7

Cardigan Bay *Sea feature* Wales, UK 69 C6

Caribbean Sea Atlantic Ocean 34-35

Carlisle England, UK 68 D4

Carlsbad New Mexico, USA 26 D3

Carlsberg Ridge *Undersea feature* Indian Ocean 112 B3

Carnarvon Australia 128 A4

Carnegie, Lake *Lake* Australia 129 C5

Carolina Brazil 41 F3

Caroline Island *Island* Kiribati 127 H3

Caroline Islands *Island group* Micronesia 126 B1

Caroní *River* Venezuela 39 F2

Carpathian Mountains *Mountain range* E Europe *var.* Carpathians 61 E4

Carpathians *see* Carpathian Mountains

Carpaţii Meridionali *Mountain range* Romania *Eng.* South Carpathians, Transylvanian Alps 88 B4

Carpentaria, Gulf of *Sea feature* Australia 126 A4

Carson City Nevada, USA 25 C5

Cartagena Colombia 38 B1

Cartagena Spain 73 F4

Cartago Costa Rica 33 E4

Cartwright Canada 19 G2

Carúpano Venezuela 39 E1

Casablanca Morocco 50 C2

Casa Grande Arizona, USA 26 3

Cascade Range *Mountain range* Canada/USA 24 B3

Cascais Portugal 72 B4

Caseyr, Raas *Coastal feature* Somalia 48 E4

Casper Wyoming, USA 22 C3

Caspian Sea *Inland sea* Asia/Europe 94 A4

Castellón de la Plana Spain 73 F3

Castelo Branco Portugal 72 C3

Castries *Capital of* St Lucia 35 G4

Castro Chile 45 B6

Cat Island *Island* Bahamas 34 D1

Catania Italy 77 D7

Catanzaro Italy 77 D6

Cauca *River* Colombia 38 B2

Caucasus *Mountains* Asia/Europe 61 G4 92 B2

Cauquenes Chile 44 B4

Caura *River* Venezuela 39 E2

Caviana, Ilha *Island* Brazil 41 F1

Cawnpore *see* Kānpur

Caxias do Sul Brazil 42 D4

Cayenne *Capital of* French Guiana 39 H3

Cayman Islands *External territory* UK, West Indies 34

Cayman Trench *Undersea feature* Caribbean Sea 34 B3

Cebu Philippines 121 E2

Cedar Rapids Iowa, USA 23 G3

Cedros, Isla *Island* Mexico 30 A2

Cefalù Italy 77 C7

Celebes *see* Sulawesi

Celebes Sea Pacific Ocean *Ind.* Laut Sulawesi 122 B3

Celje Slovenia 80 A2

Central African Republic *Country* C Africa *abbrev.* CAR 56-57

Central Makrān Range *Mountains* Pakistan 114 A3

Central Russian Upland *Upland* Russian Federation 92 B3

Central Siberian Plateau *Plateau* Russian Federation 95 E3

Cephalonia *see* Kefallonía

Cernăuţi *see* Chernivtsi

Cēsis Latvia *Ger.* Wenden 86 C3

České Budějovice Czech Republic *Ger.* Budweis 79 B5

Ceuta *External territory* Spain, N Africa 50 C1

Cévennes *Mountains* France 71 C6

Ceylon *see* Sri Lanka

Ceylon Plain *Undersea feature* Indian Ocean 117 F4

Chad *Country* C Africa 56

Chad, Lake *Lake* C Africa 48 C4

Chāgai Hills *Mountains* Pakistan 114 A2

Chalándri Greece 85 C5

Chalkída Greece 85 C5

Châlons-sur-Marne France 70 D3

Chambéry France 71 D5

Champlaim Seamount *Undersea feature* Atlantic Ocean 43 G1

Chañaral Chile 44 B2

Chandīgarh India 112 D2

Chang, Ko *Island* Thailand 119 C5

Changchun China 108 D3

Chang Jiang *River* China *var.* Yangtze 104 D4 109 B5

Changsha China 109 C6

Changzhi China 109 C6

Chaniá Greece 85 C7

Channel Islands *Islands* UK 69 D8

Channel-Port-aux-Basques Canada 19 G4

Channel Tunnel France/UK 69 E7

Chapala, Lago de *Lake* Mexico 30 D4

Chardzhev Turkmenistan *prev.* Chardzhou, *prev.* Leninsk, *Turkm.* Chärjew 102 D3

Chardzhou *see* Chardzhev

Chari *River* C Africa 56 C3

Chārīkār Afghanistan 103 E4

Chärjew *see* Chardzhev

Charleroi Belgium 67 C7

Charleston South Carolina, USA 29 F2

Charleston West Virginia, USA 20 D5

Clermont-Ferrand France 71 C5
Cleveland Ohio, USA 20 D3
Clipperton Island *External territory* France, Pacific Ocean 123 F3
Cloncurry Australia 126 B5 130 A1
Clovis New Mexico, USA 27 E2
Cluj-Napoca Romania 88 B3
Coast Mountains *Mountain range* Canada 14 C2
Coast Ranges *Mountain range* W USA 24 A3
Coats Island *Island* Canada 18 C1
Coatzacoalcos Mexico 31 G4
Cobán Guatemala 32 B2
Cochabamba Bolivia 40 C4
Cochin India 116 C5
Cochrane Canada 18 C4
Cochrane Chile 45 B6
Coco *River* Honduras/Nicaragua 32 D2
Cocos (Keeling) Islands *External territory* Australia, Indian Ocean 112 D4
Cod, Cape *Coastal feature* NE USA 15 F3 21 G3
Coeur d'Alene Idaho, USA 24 C2
Coffs Harbour Australia 130 C2
Coihaique Chile 45 B6
Coimbatore India 116 D3
Coimbra Portugal 72 C3
Colbeck, Cape *Coastal feature* Antarctica 132 C4
Colchester England, UK 69 E6
Colhué Huapi, Lago *Lake* Argentina 45 B6
Colima *Peak* Mexico 15 E5
Colmar France 70 E4
Cologne *see* Köln
Colombia *Country* N South America 38-39
Colombian Basin *Undersea feature* Caribbean Sea 34 D5
Colombo *Capital of* Sri Lanka 117 E3
Colón, Archipiélago de *see* Galapagos Islands
Colorado *State* USA 22 C5
Colorado *River* USA 14 D3
Colorado *River* Argentina 45 C5

Colorado Plateau *Upland region* S USA 26 B1
Colorado Springs Colorado, USA 22 D4
Columbia South Carolina, USA 29 F2
Columbia *River* NW USA 24 C1
Columbus Georgia, USA 28 D3
Columbus Mississippi, USA 28 C2
Columbus Nebraska, USA 23 E4
Columbus Ohio, USA 20 D4
Comayagua Honduras 32 C2
Comilla Bangladesh 115 G4
Communism Peak *Peak* Tajikistan *Rus.* Pik Kommunizma, *prev.* Stalin Peak, Garmo Peak 92 C4
Como, Lago di *Lake* Italy 76 B2
Comodoro Rivadavia Argentina 45 C6
Comoros *Country* Indian Ocean 59
Conakry *Capital of* Guinea 52 C4
Concepción Chile 45 B5
Concepción Paraguay 42 B2
Conchos *River* Mexico 30 C2
Concord California, USA 25 B6
Concord New Hampshire, USA 20 G2
Concordia E Argentina 44 D3
Congo *Country* C Africa 57
Congo *River* C Africa *var.* Zaire 49 C5
Congo Basin *Drainage basin* C Africa 49 C5
Connecticut *State* USA 21 G3
Constance, Lake *River* C Europe 75 B7
Constantine Algeria 51 E1
Constantinople *see* İstanbul
Constanţa Romania 88 D5
Coober Pedy Australia 129 E5
Cook, Mount *Peak* New Zealand *prev.* Aorangi 125 E5
Cook Islands *External territory* New Zealand, Pacific Ocean 122 D4
Cook Strait *Sea feature* New Zealand 125 D5
Cooktown Australia 126 B4
Coos Bay Oregon, USA 24 A3

Copenhagen *Capital of* Denmark 65 B7
Copiapó Chile 44 B3
Coppermine Canada 17 E3
Coquimbo Chile 44 B3
Corabia Romania 88 B5
Coral Sea Pacific Ocean 122 C3
Coral Sea Islands *External territory* Australia, Coral Sea 126 C4
Corantijn *River* Guyana/Surinam *var.* Courantyne 39 C3
Cordillera Cantábrica *Mountain range* Spain 72 D1
Córdoba Argentina 44 C3
Córdoba Spain 72 D4
Cordova Alaska, USA 16 D3
Corfu *see* Kérkyra
Corinth *see* Kórinthos
Corinth, Gulf of *see* Korinthiakós Kólpos
Corinto Nicaragua 32 C3
Cork Ireland 69 A6
Corner Brook Canada 19 G3
Coro Venezuela 38 D1
Coromandel New Zealand 131 G2
Coronel Oviedo Paraguay 42 C2
Corpus Christi Texas, USA 27 G4
Corrib, Lough *Lake* Ireland 69 A5
Corrientes Argentina 44 D3
Corse *Island* France *Eng.* Corsica 71 E7 82 D2
Corsica *see* Corse
Çorum Turkey 96 D2
Corvallis Oregon, USA 24 A3
Cosenza Italy 77 D6
Costa Blanca *Coastal region* Spain 73 F4
Costa Brava *Coastal region* Spain 73 H2
Costa Rica *Country* Central America 32-33
Côte d'Ivoire *see* Ivory Coast
Cotonou Benin 53 F5
Cotopaxi *Peak* Ecuador 36 B2
Cottbus Germany 74 D4
Council Bluffs Iowa, USA 23 F4

Courantyne *River*
Guyana/Surinam
var. Corantijn 39 G3

Courland Lagoon *Sea feature*
Baltic Sea 86 A4

Coventry England, UK 69 D6

Covilhã Portugal 72 C3

Cozumel, Isla de *Island* Mexico
31 H3

Cracow *see* Kraków

Craiova Romania 88 B5

Cremona Italy 76 B2

Cres Island Croatia 80 A3

Crescent City California, USA
24 A4

Crete Greece *see* Kríti 83 F4

Crete, Sea of Mediterranean Sea
Gk. Kritikó Pélagos 85 D5

Crimea *Peninsula* Ukraine
var. Krym 88 F4

Croatia *Country* SE Europe 80

Croker Island *Island* Australia
128 D2

Crotone Italy 77 E6

Crozet Basin *Undersea feature*
Indian Ocean 113 B6

Crozet Islands *Island group*
Indian Ocean 113 B6

Cruzeiro do Sul Brazil 40 B3

Cuanza *River* Angola 58 B1

Cuba *Country* West Indies 34

Cubango *see* Okavango

Cúcuta Colombia 38 C2

Cuenca Ecuador 38 A5

Cuenca Spain 73 E3

Cuernavaca Mexico 31 E4

Cuiabá Brazil 41 E4

Cuito *River* Angola 58 C2

Culiacán Mexico 30 C3

Cumaná Venezuela 39 E1

Cumberland Maryland, USA
21 E4

Cumberland *River* C USA 20 C5

Cunene *River* Angola/Namibia
58 B2

Cunnamulla Australia 130 B2

Curicó Chile 44 B4

Curitiba Brazil 42 D3

Cusco Peru *prev.* Cuzco 40 B4

Cuttack India 115 F5

Cuxhaven Germany 74 B3

Cuyuni *River*
Guyana/Venezuela 39 F2

Cuzco *see* Cusco

Cyclades *see* Kykládes

Cymru *see* Wales

Cyprus *Country* Mediterranean
Sea 96 C5

Czechoslovakia *see* Czech
Republic *or* Slovakia

Czech Republic *Country*
C Europe 78-79

Częstochowa Poland
Ger. Tschenstochau 78 C4

D

Dacca *see* Dhaka

Dagden *see* Hiiumaa

Dagö *see* Hiiumaa

Dagupan Philippines 121 E1

Da Hinggan Ling *Mountain
range* China *Eng.* Great
Khingan Range 107 G1

Dahomey *see* Benin

Dakar *Capital of* Senegal 52 B3

Đakovo Croatia 80 C3

Dalaman Turkey 96 B4

Đa Lat Vietnam 119 E5

Dali China 109 A6

Dalian China 108 D4

Dallas Texas, USA 27 G3

Dalmacija *Region* Croatia
80 B4

Daloa Ivory Coast 52 D5

Daly Waters Australia 128 E3

Damán India 114 C5

Damas *see* Damascus

Damascus Syria *var.* Esh Sham,
Fr. Damas, *Ar.* Dimashq 98 B4

Dampier Australia 128 B4

Đa Nang Vietnam 119 E4

Daneborg Greenland 63 E3

Dangara Tajikistan 103 E3

Danmarkshavn Greenland 63 E2

Danmarksstraedet *see* Denmark
Strait

Danube *River* C Europe 60 D4

Danube Delta *Wetland*
Romania/Ukraine 88 D5

Danville Virginia, USA 21 E5

Danzig *see* Gdańsk

Dar'ā Syria 99 B5

Dardanelles *Sea feature* Turkey
Turk. Çanakkale Boğazı 96 A2

Dar es Salaam Tanzania 55 C8

Darhan Mongolia 107 E2

Darien, Gulf of *Sea feature*
Caribbean Sea 33 G5

Darling *River* Australia 130 B2

Darmstadt Germany 75 B5

Darnah Libya 51 H2

Darnley, Cape *Coastal feature*
Antarctica 133 G2

Dartmoor *Region* England, UK
69 C7

Dartmouth Canada 19 G4

Darwin Australia 128 D2

Dashhowuz *see* Dashkhovuz

Dashkhovuz Turkmenistan
prev. Tashauz, *Turkm.*
Dashhowuz 102 C2

Datong China 108 C4

Daugava *see* Western Dvina

Daugavpils Latvia *Ger.*
Dünaburg, *Rus.* Dvinsk 86 C4

Dāvangere India 116 D2

Davao Philippines 121 F2

Davenport Iowa, USA 23 G3

David Panama 33 E5

Davis Sea Indian Ocean 133 H3

Davis Strait *Sea feature* Atlantic
Ocean 17 H2 62 A4

Dawson Canada 16 D3

Dayr az Zawr Syria 98 D3

Dayton Ohio, USA 20 C4

Daytona Beach Florida, USA
29 F4

Dead Sea *Salt Lake* SW Asia
Ar. Al Baḥr al Mayyit, Baḥrat
Lūṭ, *Heb.* Yam HaMelaḥ 99 B5

Death Valley *Valley* W USA
14 D4 25 D6

Debre Zeyit Ethiopia 55 C5

Debrecen Hungary *prev.*
Debreczen, *Ger.* Debreczin
79 D6

Debreczen *see* Debrecen

Debreczin *see* Debrecen

Decatur Illinois, USA 20 B4

Deccan *Plateau* India 104 B3

Děčín Czech Republic
Ger. Tetschen 78 B4

Dej Romania 88 B3

Delaware *State* USA 21 F4

Delaware Bay *Sea feature* USA
21 F4

Delémont Switzerland 75 A7

Drobeta-Turnu Severin Romania
prev. Turnu Severin 88 B4
Druskieniki see Druskininkai
Druskininkai Lithuania
Pol. Druskieniki 87 B5
Dubai United Arab Emirates
101 D5
Dubăsari Moldavia 88 D3
Dubawnt River Canada 17 F4
Dubbo Australia 130 C3
Dublin Capital of Ireland 69 B5
Dubrovnik Croatia 81 C5
Dubuque Iowa, USA 23 G3
Duero River Portugal/Spain
Port. Douro 72 D2
Dugi Otok Island Croatia
80 A4
Duisburg Germany 74 A4
Duluth Minnesota, USA 23 F2
Dumfries Scotland, UK 68 C4
Düna see Western Dvina
Dünaburg see Daugavpils
Dundalk Ireland 69 B5
Dundee Scotland, UK 68 C3
Dunedin New Zealand 131 F5
Dunkerque France
Eng. Dunkirk 70 C2
Dunkirk see Dunkerque
Duqm Oman 101 E6
Durango Mexico 30 D3
Durango Colorado, USA 22 C5
Durazno Uruguay 42 C5
Durban South Africa 58 E4
Durham North Carolina, USA
29 F1
Durrës Albania 81 C6
Dushanbe Capital of Tajikistan
var. Dyushambe,
prev. Stalinabad 103 E3
Düsseldorf Germany 74 A4
Dutch Harbor Alaska, USA
16 B3
Dutch West Indies see
Netherland Antilles
Dvina River E Europe 61 E3
Dvinsk see Daugavpils
Dyushambe see Dushanbe
Dzaudzhikau see Vladikavkaz
Dzhalal-Abad Kyrgyzstan
Kir. Jalal-Abad 103 F2
Dzhambul see Zhambyl
Dzhezkazgan see Zhezkazgan

Dzhugdzhur Range Mountain
range Russian Federation
93 F3
Dzvina see Western Dvina

E

Eagle Pass Texas, USA 27 F4
East Cape Coastal feature New
Zealand 131 H2
East China Sea Pacific Ocean
122 B2
Easter Island Island Pacific
Ocean 123 F4
Eastern Ghats Mountain range
India 104 B4
Eastern Sierra Madre see Sierra
Madre Oriental
East Falkland Island Falkland
Islands 45 D7
East Frisian Islands see
Ostfriesische Inseln
East London South Africa 58 D5
Eastmain River Canada 18 D3
East Pacific Rise Undersea feature
Pacific Ocean 123 F3
East Siberian Sea see Vostochno-
Sibirskoye More
East St Louis Illinois, USA 20 B4
Eau Claire Wisconsin, USA
20 A2
Ebolowa Cameroon 57 B5
Ebro River Spain 73 F2
Ecuador Country NW South
America 38
Ed Eritrea 54 D4
Ede Netherlands 66 D3
Ede Nigeria 53 F4
Edgeøya Island Svalbard 63 H2
Edinburgh Scotland, UK 68 C4
Edirne Turkey 96 A2
Edmonton Canada 17 E5
Edward, Lake Lake
Uganda/Zaire 57 E6
Edwards Plateau Upland S USA
27 F4
Eforie-Nord Romania 88 D5
Egadi, Isole Island group Italy
77 B7
Ege Denizi see Aegean Sea
Eger see Ohře
Egiyn Gol River Mongolia 106
D2

Egypt Country NE Africa 54
Eindhoven Netherlands 67 D5
Eisenstadt Austria 75 E7
Eivissa Island Spain Cast. Ibiza
73 G4
Elat Israel 99 B7
Elâziğ Turkey 97 E3
Elba, Isola d' Island Italy
76 B4
Elbasan Albania 81 D6
Elbe River Czech
Republic/Germany 79 B5
Elbing see Elblag
Elblag Poland Ger. Elbing 78 C2
El'brus Peak Russian Federation
61 G4 83 H2
Elche Spain 73 F4
Elda Spain 73 F4
Eldoret Kenya 55 C6
Eleuthera Island Bahamas
34 C1
El Fasher Sudan var. Al Fāshir
54 A4
Elgin Scotland, UK 68 C3
El Gîza Egypt var. Al Jīzah
54 B1
Elista Russian Federation 91 B7
El Khârga Egypt
var. Al Khārijah 54 B2
Elko Nevada, USA 25 D5
Ellensburg Washington, USA
24 B2
Ellesmere Island Island Canada
17 F1
Ellsworth Land Region
Antarctica 132 B3
El Minya Egypt 54 B2
Elmira New York, USA 21 E3
El Obeid Sudan 54 B4
El Paso Texas, USA 26 D3
El Qâhira see Cairo
El Salvador Country Central
America 32
El Tigre Venezuela 39 E2
Ely NV USA 25 D5
Emden Germany 74 A3
Emmen Netherlands 66 E2
Emperor Seamount Undersea
feature Pacific Ocean 122 D2
Empty Quarter see Rub' al Khali
Ems River Germany/
Netherlands 74 A3
Encarnación Paraguay 42 C3

Finisterre, Cape *Coastal feature* Spain 72 B1

Finland *Country* N Europe 64-65

Finland, Gulf of *Sea feature* Baltic Sea 65 E6

Firenze Italy *Eng.* Florence 76 B3

Fish *River* Namibia 58 C4

Fishguard Wales, UK 69 C6

Fitzroy *River* Australia 124 B2 128 C3

Fiume *see* Rijeka

Flagstaff Arizona, USA 26 B2

Flanders *Region* Belgium 67 A5

Flensburg Germany 74 B2

Flinders Island *Island* Australia 130 B4

Flinders Ranges *Mountain range* Australia 130 A2

Flin Flon Canada 17 F5

Flint Michigan, USA 20 C3

Flint Island *Island* Kiribati 127 H4

Florence Alabama, USA 28 C2

Florence South Carolina, USA 29 F2

Florence *see* Firenze

Florencia Colombia 38 B3

Flores Guatemala 32 B1

Flores *Island* Indonesia 121 E5

Flores, Laut *see* Flores Sea

Flores Sea Pacific Ocean *Ind.* Laut Flores 121 E5

Florianópolis Brazil 42 D3

Florida *State* USA 29 E4

Florida, Straits of *Sea feature* Bahamas/USA 29 F5 34 B1

Floridablanca Colombia 38 C2

Florida Keys *Island chain* Florida, USA 29 F5

Flórina Greece 84 A3

Flushing *see* Vlissingen

Foča Bosnia & Herzegovina 80 C4

Focşani Romania 88 C4

Foggia Italy 77 D5

Fongafale *Capital of* Tuvalu 127 E3

Fonseca, Gulf of *Sea feature* El Salvador/Honduras 32 C3

Forlì Italy 76 C3

Formentera *Island* Spain 73 G4

Former Yugoslav Republic of Macedonia *see* Macedonia

Formosa Argentina 44 D2

Formosa *see* Taiwan

Formosa Strait *see* Taiwan Strait

Fóroyar *see* Faeroe Islands

Fortaleza Brazil 41 H2

Fort Collins Colorado, USA 22 D4

Fort-de-France *Capital of* Martinique 35 G4

Forth *River* Scotland, UK 68 C4

Forth, Firth of *Inlet* Scotland, UK 68 D4

Fort Lauderdale Florida, USA 29 F5

Fort McMurray Canada 17 F4

Fort Myers Florida, USA 29 E5

Fort Peck Lake *Lake* Montana, USA 22 C1

Fort Saint John Canada 17 E4

Fort Smith Canada 17 F4

Fort Smith Arkansas, USA 28 A1

Fort Wayne Indiana, USA 20 C4

Fort William Scotland, UK 68 C3

Fort Worth Texas, USA 27 G3

Foveaux Strait *Sea feature* New Zealand 131 B5

Fram Basin *Undersea feature* Arctic Ocean *var.* Ángara Basin 12 C4

Franca Brazil 43 E1

France *Country* W Europe 70-71

Francistown Botswana 58 D3

Frankfort Kentucky, USA 20 C5

Frankfurt *see* Frankfurt am Main

Frankfurt am Main Germany *Eng.* Frankfurt 75 B5

Frankfurt an der Oder Germany 74 D4

Fränkische Alb *Mountains* Germany 75 C6

Frantsa-Iosifa, Zemlya *Islands* Russian Federation *Eng.* Franz Josef Land 13 D6 94 D1

Franz Josef Land *see* Frantsa-Iosifa, Zemlya

Fraser Island *Island* Australia 130 D1

Frauenburg *see* Saldus

Fray Bentos Uruguay 42 B5

Fredericton Canada 19 F4

Frederikshavn Denmark 65 B7

Fredrikstad Norway 65 B6

Freeport Bahamas 34 C1

Freeport Texas, USA 27 G4

Freetown *Capital of* Sierra Leone 52 C4

Freiburg im Breisgau Germany 75 B7

Fremantle Australia 129 B6

French Guiana *External territory* France, N South America 39

French Polynesia *External territory* France, Pacific Ocean 123 E3

Fresno California, USA 25 B6

Fribourg Switzerland 75 A7

Frome, Lake *Salt lake* Australia 130 A2

Frosinone Italy 76 C4

Frunze *see* Bishkek

Fuerteventura *Island* Spain 50 A3

Fuji, Mount *Peak* Japan 105 E2

Fukui Japan 111 C5

Fukuoka Japan 111 A6

Fukushima Japan 110 D3

Fulda Germany 75 B5

Fünfkirchen *see* Pécs

Furnas, Represa de *Reservoir* Brazil 43 E1

Fuzhou China 109 D6

FYR Macedonia *see* Macedonia

G

Gaalkacyo Somalia 55 E5

Gabès Tunisia 51 E2

Gabon *Country* W Africa 57

Gaborone *Capital of* Botswana 58 D4

Gadsden Alabama, USA 28 D2

Gaeta, Golfo di *Sea feature* Italy 77 C5

Gafsa Tunisia 51 E2

Gagnoa Ivory Coast 52 D5

Gagra Georgia 97 E1

Gairdner, Lake *Lake* Australia 129 E6

Gold Coast *Coastal region* Australia 130 D2

Goldingen *see* Kuldīga

Golmud China 106 D4

Goma Zaire 57 E6

Gomel' *see* Homyel'

Gómez Palacio Mexico 30 D2

Gonaïves Haiti 34 D3

Gonder Ethiopia 54 C4

Good Hope, Cape of *Coastal feature* South Africa 58 C5

Goodiwindi Australia 130 C2

Goose Lake *Lake* W USA 24 B4

Goré Chad 56 C4

Gorē Ethiopia 55 C5

Gorgān Iran 100 D3

Gorki *see* Horki

Gor'kiy *see* Nizhniy Novgorod

Gorlovka *see* Horlivka

Gorontalo Indonesia 121 E4

Gorzów Wielkopolski Poland *Ger.* Landsberg 78 B3

Gospić Croatia 80 A3

Gostivar Macedonia 81 D5

Göteborg Sweden 65 B7

Gotland *Island* Sweden 65 C7

Gotō-rettō *Island group* Japan 111 A6

Göttingen Germany 74 B4

Gouda Netherlands 66 C4

Gough Island *External territory* UK, Atlantic Ocean 47 D6

Gouin, Réservoir *Reservoir* Canada 18 D4

Governador Valadares Brazil 41 G4 43 F1

Gozo *Island* Malta 77 C8

Gračanica Bosnia & Herzegovina 80 C3

Grafton Australia 130 D2

Graham Land *Region* Antarctica 132 B3

Grampian Mountains *Mountains* Scotland, UK 68 C3

Granada Nicaragua 32 D3

Granada Spain 73 E4

Gran Canaria *Island* Spain 50 A3

Gran Chaco *Region* C South America 34 C4

Grand Bahama *Island* Bahamas 34 C1

Grand Banks *Undersea feature* Atlantic Ocean 46 B3

Grand Canyon *Valley* SW USA 26 B1

Grande, Bahía *Sea feature* Argentina 37 C7

Grande, Rio *River* Brazil 42 D4 43 E1

Grande Comore *Island* Comoros 59 F2

Grande Prairie Canada 17 E5

Grand Erg Occidental *Desert region* Algeria 50 D2

Grand Erg Oriental *Desert region* Algeria/Tunisia 51 E3

Grand Falls Canada 19 H3

Grand Forks North Dakota, USA 23 E1

Grand Junction Colorado, USA 22 C4

Grand Rapids Michigan, USA 20 C3

Graudenz *see* Grudziądz

Graz Austria 75 E7

Great Abaco *Island* Bahamas 34 C1

Great Ararat *see* Ararat, Mount

Great Australian Bight *Sea feature* Australia 122 B4 129 D6

Great Bahama Bank *Undersea feature* Atlantic Ocean 34 C2

Great Barrier Reef *Coral reef* Coral Sea 122 C4

Great Basin *Region* USA 24 D4

Great Bear Lake *Lake* Canada 17 E3

Great Dividing Range *Mountain range* Australia 124 D3

Greater Antarctica *Region* Antarctica 133 F3

Greater Antilles *Island group* West Indies 34 C3

Great Exuma Island *Island* Bahamas 34 C2

Great Falls Montana, USA 22 B1

Great Inagua *Island* Bahamas 34 D2

Great Khingan Range *see* Da Hinggan Ling

Great Lakes, The *Lakes* N America *incl.* Erie, Huron, Michigan, Ontario, Superior 15 F3

Great Nicobar *Island* India 117 H3

Great Plain of China *Region* China 104 D2

Great Plains *Region* N America 14 D3

Great Rift Valley *Valley* E Africa/SW Asia 55 C6

Great Salt Lake *Salt lake* Utah, USA 22 B3

Great Sand Sea *Desert region* Egypt/Libya 51 H3

Great Sandy Desert *Desert* Australia 128 C4

Great Sandy Desert *see* Rub' al Khali

Great Slave Lake *Lake* Canada 17 F4

Great Victoria Desert *Desert* Australia 129 C5

Gredos, Sierra de *Mountains* Spain 72 D3

Greece *Country* SE Europe 84-85

Green Bay Wisconsin, USA 20 B2

Greenland *External territory* Denmark, Atlantic Ocean *var.* Grønland 62

Greenland Basin *Undersea feature* Atlantic Ocean 63 F2

Greenland Sea Atlantic Ocean 63 F2

Greenock Scotland, UK 68 C4

Greensboro North Carolina, USA 29 F1

Greenville South Carolina, USA 29 E2

Greifswald Germany 74 D2

Grenada *Country* West Indies 35 G5

Grenoble France 71 D5

Greymouth New Zealand 131 F3

Grimsby England, UK 69 E5

Grodno *see* Hrodna

Groningen Netherlands 66 E1

Grønland *see* Greenland

Grootfontein Namibia 58 C3

Grosseto Italy 76 B4

Grosskanizsa *see* Nagykanizsa

Groznyy Russian Federation 91 B7 94 A4

Grudziądz Poland *Ger.* Graudenz 78 C3

Grünberg in Schlesien *see* Zielona Góra

Guadalajara Mexico 30 D4

Hattiesburg Mississippi, USA 28 C3

Hat Yai Thailand 119 C7

Haugesund Norway 65 A6

Havana *Capital of* Cuba *Sp.* La Habana 34 B2

Havre Montana, USA 22 C1

Havre-Saint-Pierre Canada 19 F3

Hawaii *State* USA 123 E2

Hawaiian Islands *Islands* USA 93 H4

Hawlêr *see* Arbîl

Hawthorne Nevada, USA 25 C6

Hay River Canada 17 E4

Hays Kansas, USA 23 E4

Heard Island *Island* Indian Ocean 113 C7

Heerenveen Netherlands 66 D2

Heerlen Netherlands 67 D6

Hefa Israel *prev.* Haifa 99 A5

Hefei China 109 D5

Heidelberg Germany 75 B6

Heilbronn Germany 75 B6

Helena Montana, USA 22 B2

Helmand *River* Afghanistan 102 C5

Helmond Netherlands 67 D5

Helsingborg Sweden 65 B7

Helsingør Denmark 65 B7

Helsinki *Capital of* Finland 65 D6

Helwân Egypt 54 B1

Hengelo Netherlands 66 E3

Henzada Burma 118 A4

Herât Afghanistan 102 C4

Hermansverk Norway 65 A5

Hermosillo Mexico 30 B2

Herning Denmark 65 A7

Hialeah Florida, USA 29 F5

Hiiumaa *Island* Estonia *Ger.* Dagden, *Swed.* Dagö 86 C2

Hildesheim Germany 74 B4

Hilla *see* Al Ḥillah

Hilversum Netherlands 66 C3

Himalayas *Mountain range* S Asia 104 D2

Himora Ethiopia 54 C4

Ḥimṣ Syria 98 B3

Hindu Kush *Mountain range* C Asia 103 E4

Hiroshima Japan 111 B5

Hitachi Japan 110 D4

Hjørring Denmark 65 A7

Hlybokaye Belorussia *Rus.* Glubokoye 87 D5

Hobart Tasmania 130 B5

Hobbs New Mexico, USA 5627 E3

Hô Chi Minh Vietnam *var.* Ho Chi Minh City, *prev.* Saigon 119 E6

Ho Chi Minh City *see* Hô Chi Minh

Hodeida *see* Al Ḥudaydah

Hoek van Holland Netherlands 66 B4

Hoggar *see* Ahaggar

Hohhot China 107 F3

Hokkaidô *Island* Japan 110 D2

Holguín Cuba 34 C2

Hollywood Florida, USA 29 F5

Holland *see* Netherlands

Holon Israel 99 A5

Holyhead Wales, UK 69 C5

Homyel' Belorussia *Rus.* Gomel' 87 D7

Honduras *Country* Central America 32-33

Honduras, Gulf of *Sea feature* Caribbean Sea 32 C2

Hønefoss Norway 65 B6

Hông Gai Vietnam 118 E3

Hong Kong *External territory* UK, E Asia 109 C7

Hongze Hu *Lake* China 109 D5

Honiara *Capital of* Solomon Islands 126 C3

Honolulu Hawaii, USA 123 E2

Honshû *Island* Japan 110 D3

Honshu Ridge *Undersea feature* Pacific Ocean 105 F2

Hoorn Netherlands 66 C2

Hopa Turkey 97 F2

Hopedale Canada 19 F2

Hopkinsville Kentucky, USA 20 B5

Horki Belorussia *Rus.* Gorki 87 E6

Horlivka Ukraine *Rus.* Gorlovka 88 G3

Horn, Cape *Coastal feature* Chile 45 C8

Horog *see* Khorog

Horsens Denmark 65 A7

Hotan China 106 B4

Hot Springs Arkansas, USA 28 B2

Hotspur Seamount *Undersea feature* Atlantic Ocean 41 H5 43 H1

Hô Thac Ba *Lake* Vietnam 118 D3

Houston Texas, USA 27 G4

Hovd Mongolia 106 C2

Hövsgöl Nuur *Lake* Mongolia 106 D1

Howe, Cape *Coastal feature* Australia 124 D4 130 C4

Hradec Králové Czech Republic *Ger.* Königgrätz 79 B5

Hrodna Belorussia *Rus.* Grodno 87 B5

Huacho Peru 40 A3

Huainan China 109 D5

Huambo Angola 58 B2

Huancayo Peru 40 B4

Huang He *River* China *Eng.* Yellow River 104 D2 107 F4 108 C4

Huánuco Peru 40 B4

Huaraz Peru 40 B3

Huascarán *Peak* Peru 36 B3

Hubli India 116 C2

Hudson *River* NE USA 21 F3

Hudson Bay *Sea feature* Canada 15 E2

Hudson Strait *Sea feature* Canada 15 F2

Huê Vietnam 118 E4

Huehuetenango Guatemala 32 B2

Huelva Spain 72 C4

Huesca Spain 73 F2

Hughenden Australia 130 B1

Hull *see* Kingston upon Hull

Hulun Nur *Lake* China 107 F1

Humboldt *River* W USA 25 C5

Hungarian Plain *Plain* C Europe 83 E1

Hungary *Country* C Europe 79

Huntington West Virginia, USA 20 D5

Huntsville Alabama, USA 28 D2

Hurghada Egypt 54 B2

Huron, Lake *Lake* Canada/USA 15 F3

Húsavík Iceland 63 E4
Huvadhu Atoll *Island* Maldives 116 C5
Hvar *Island* Croatia 80 B4
Hyargas Nuur *Lake* Mongolia 106 C2
Hyderābād India 114 B3 116 D1
Hyères, Îles d' *Islands* France 71 D6

I

Iaşi Romania 88 D3
Ibadan Nigeria 53 F5
Ibagué Colombia 38 B3
Ibarra Ecuador 38 A4
Iberian Peninsula *Peninsula* SW Europe 46 D3 82 D3
Ibiza *see* Eivissa
Ica Peru 40 B4
İçel *see* Mersin
Iceland *Country* Atlantic Ocean 63 E4
Idaho *State* USA 24
Idaho Falls Idaho, USA 24 E3
Idfu Egypt 54 B2
Idlib Syria 98 B2
Ieper Belgium *Fr.* Ypres 67 A6
Ifôghas, Adrar des *Upland* Mali *var.* Adrar des Iforas 53 F2
Iforas, Adrar des *see* Ifôghas, Adrar des
Iglau *see* Jihlava
Iglesias Italy 77 A5
Ihosy Madagascar 59 G3
Iisalmi Finland 64 E4
Ijebu-Ode Nigeria 53 F5
IJssel *River* Netherlands 66 D3
IJsselmeer *Lake* Netherlands *prev.* Zuider Zee 66 D2
Ikaría *Island* Greece 85 D5
Iki *Island* Japan 111 A6
Ilagan Philippines 121 E1
Ilebo Zaire 57 C6
Iligan Philippines 121 E2
Illapel Chile 44 B3
Illinois *State* USA 20 B4
Iloilo Philippines 121 E2
Ilorin Nigeria 53 F4
Íluh *see* Batman
Ilulissat Greenland 62 B3

Imatra Finland 65 E5
Imperatriz Brazil 41 F2
Impfondo Congo 57 C5
Imphāl India 115 H4
Independence Missouri, USA 23 F4
Independence Fjord *Inlet* Greenland 62 D1
India *Country* S Asia 114-115 116-117
Indian Ocean 112-113
Indiana *State* USA 20 C4
Indianapolis Indiana, USA 20 C4
Indonesia *Country* SE Asia 120-121
Indore India 114 D4
Indus *River* S Asia 114 C1
Indus Delta *Wetlands* Pakistan 114 B4
Inglefield Land *Region* Greenland 62 A2
Ingolstadt Germany 75 E6
Inguri *see* Enguri
Inhambane Mozambique 59 E3
Inn *River* C Europe 75 D6
Inner Islands *Islands* Seychelles 59 H1
Inner Mongolia *Autonomous region* China 107 F3
Innsbruck Austria 75 C7
In Salah Algeria 50 D3
Insein Burma 118 B4
Interlaken Switzerland 75 B7
Inukjuak Canada 18 D2
Inuvik Canada 17 E3
Invercargill New Zealand 131 F5
Inverness Scotland, UK 68 C3
Ioánnina Greece 84 A4
Ionian Islands *see* Iónioi Nísoi
Ionian Sea Mediterranean Sea 83 E3
Iónioi Nísoi *Island group* Greece *Eng.* Ionian Islands 85 A5
Íos *Island* Greece 85 D6
Iowa *State* USA 23 F3
Ipoh Malaysia 120 B3
Ipswich Australia 130 C2
Ipswich England, UK 69 E6
Iqaluit Canada 17 H3
Iquique Chile 44 B1

Iquitos Peru 40 B2
Irákleio Greece 85 D7
Iran *Country* SW Asia 100-101
Iranian Plateau *Upland* Iran 100 D3
Irānshahr Iran 100 E4
Irapuato Mexico 31 E4
Iraq *Country* SW Asia 100 B3
Irbid Jordan 99 B5
Ireland *Country* W Europe 68-69
Irian Jaya *Province* Indonesia 121 H4
Iringa Tanzania 55 C7
Irish Sea British Isles 69 C5
Irkutsk Russian Federation 95 E4
Irrawaddy *River* Burma 118 B2
Irrawaddy Delta *Wetlands* Burma 118 A4
Ísafjördhur Iceland 62 D4
Ischia, Isola d' *Island* Italy 77 C5
Ishikari *River* Japan 110 D2
Isiro Zaire 57 E5
İskenderun Turkey *Eng.* Alexandretta 96 D4
Iskŭr *River* Bulgaria 84 C1
Iskŭr, Yazovir *Reservoir* Bulgaria 84 C2
Islay *Island* Scotland, UK 68 B4
Islāmābād *Capital of* Pakistan 114 C1
Ismaila *see* Ismâ'ilîya
Ismâ'ilîya Egypt *Eng.* Ismaila 54 B1
Isna Egypt 54 B2
Isparta Turkey 96 B4
Israel *Country* SW Asia 98-99
Issyk-Kul' Kyrgyzstan *prev.* Rybach'ye, *Kir.* Ysyk-Köl 103 G2
Issyk-Kul, Ozero *Lake* Kyrgyzstan 103 G2
İstanbul Turkey *var.* Stambul, *prev.* Constantinople, Byzantium, *Bul.* Tsarigrad 96 B2
İstanbul Boğazı *see* Bosporus
Itabuna Brazil 41 G4
Itaguí Colombia 38 B2
Italy *Country* S Europe 76-77

Ittoqqortoormiit Greenland 13 H7 63 B3
Iturup *Island* Japan/Russian Federation (disputed) 110 E1
Ivanhoe Australia 130 B3
Ivano-Frankivs'k Ukraine 88 C2
Ivanovo Russian Federation 90 B4
Ivittuut Greenland 62 B4
Ivory Coast *Country* W Africa *Fr.* Côte d'Ivoire 52
Ivujivik Canada 18 D1
Iwaki Japan 110 D4
Izabal, Lago de *Lake* Guatemala 32 C2
Izhevsk Russian Federation 91 C5 94 B3
İzmir Turkey *prev.* Smyrna 96 A3
İzmit Turkey *var.* Kocaeli 96 B2
Izu-shotō *Island group* Japan 111 D6

J

Jabalpur India 114 E4
Jackson Mississippi, USA 28 C3
Jacksonville Florida, USA 29 E3
Jacksonville Texas, USA 27 G3
Jacmel Haiti 34 D3
Jaén Spain 73 E4
Jaffna Sri Lanka 117 E3
Jaipur India 114 D3
Jajce Bosnia & Herzegovina 80 B3
Jakarta *Capital of* Indonesia 120 C5
Jakobstad Finland 64 D4
Jakobstadt *see* Jēkabpils
Jalālābād Afghanistan 103 E4
Jalal-Abad *see* Dzhalal-Abad
Jalandhar India 114 D2
Jalapa Mexico 31 F4
Jamaame Somalia 55 D6
Jamaica *Country* West Indies 34
Jamāpur Bangladesh 115 G4
Jambi Indonesia 120 B4
James Bay *Sea feature* Canada 18 C3/4
Jammu *Disputed region* India/Pakistan 114 D2
Jāmnagar India 114 B4

Jan Mayen *External territory* Norway, Arctic Ocean 46 A2 63 F3
Japan *Country* E Asia 110-111
Japan, Sea of Pacific Ocean 93 F4 110 B3
Japan Trench *Undersea feature* Pacific Ocean 122 C2
Järvenpää Finland 65 D5
Jarvis Island *External territory* USA, Pacific Ocean 127 G2
Jaseur Seamount *Undersea feature* Atlantic Ocean 43 H2
Java *Island* Indonesia 120 D5
Java Sea Pacific Ocean *var.* Laut Jawa 112 D4
Java Trench *Undersea feature* Indian Ocean 112 D4
Jawa, Laut *see* Java Sea
Jayapura Indonesia 121 H4
Jedda *see* Jiddah
Jefferson City Missouri, USA 23 G4
Jēkabpils Latvia *Ger.* Jakobstadt 86 C4
Jelgava Latvia *Ger.* Mitau 86 C3
Jember Indonesia 120 D5
Jena Germany 75 C5
Jérémie Haiti 34 D3
Jerevan *see* Yerevan
Jerez de la Frontera Spain 72 D5
Jericho West Bank 99 B5
Jerid, Chott el *Salt lake* Africa 82 D4
Jersey *Island* Channel Islands 69 D8
Jerusalem *Capital of* Israel 99 B5
Jesenice Slovenia 80 A2
Jhelum Pakistan 114 C2
Jiamusi China 108 E2
Jibuti *see* Djibouti
Jiddah Saudi Arabia *Eng.* Jedda 101 A6
Jihlava Czech Republic *Ger.* Iglau 79 B5
Jilin China 108 E3
Jīma Ethiopia 55 C5
Jinan China 109 C4
Jingdezhen China 109 D6
Jining China 107 F2
Jinotega Nicaragua 32 D3
Jinsha Jiang *River* China 109 A6
Jisr ash Shughūr Syria 98 B2
Jixi China 108 E3

Jīzān Saudi Arabia 101 B6
João Pessoa Brazil 41 H3
Jodhpur India 114 C3
Joensuu Finland 65 E5
Johannesburg South Africa 58 D4
Johnson City Tennessee, USA 29 E1
Johor Bahru Malaysia 120 B3
Joinville Brazil 42 D3
Joliet Illinois, USA 20 B3
Jönköping Sweden 65 B7
Jonquière Canada 19 E4
Jordan *Country* SW Asia 98-99
Jordan *River* SW Asia 99 B5
Jos Nigeria 53 G4
Juan Fernandez, Islas *Islands* Chile 123 G4
Juàzeiro Brazil 41 G3
Juàzeiro do Norte Brazil 41 G3
Juba Sudan 55 B5
Júcar *River* Spain 73 E3
Judenburg Austria 75 D7
Juigalpa Nicaragua 32 D3
Juiz de Fora Brazil 41 G5 43 F2
Juneau Alaska, USA 16 D4
Junín Argentina 44 D4
Jura *Mountains* France/Switzerland 70 D4 75 A7
Jura *Island* Scotland, UK 68 B4
Jurbarkas Lithuania *Ger.* Jurburg, *var.* Georgenburg 86 B4
Jurburg *see* Jurbarkas
Juruá *River* Brazil/Peru 40 C2
Juticalpa Honduras 32 D2
Jutland *see* Jylland
Juventud, Isla de la *Island* Cuba 34 B2
Jylland *Peninsula* Denmark *Eng.* Jutland 65 A7
Jyväskylä Finland 65 D5

K

K2 *Peak* China/Pakistan *Eng.* Mount Godwin Austen 104 C2
Kaachka *see* Kaka
Kaakhka *see* Kaka
Kabale Uganda 55 B6

Kabalebo Reservoir *Reservoir* Surinam 39 G3

Kabinda Zaire 57 D7

Kābol *see* Kābul

Kābul *Capital of* Afghanistan *Per.* Kābol 103 E3

Kachch, Gulf of *Sea feature* Arabian Sea 114 B4

Kachch, Rann of *Wetland* India/Pakistan *var.* Rann of Kutch 114 B4

Kadugli Sudan 54 B4

Kaduna Nigeria 53 G4

Kaédi Mauritania 52 C3

Kâğıthane Turkey 96 B2

Kagoshima Japan 111 A6

Kahramanmaraş Turkey *var.* Marash, Maraş 96 D4

Kai, Kepulauan *Island group* Indonesia 120 A3

Kaikoura New Zealand 131 G3

Kainji Reservoir *Reservoir* Nigeria 53 F4

Kairouan Tunisia 51 E1

Kaitaia New Zealand 131 G1

Kajaani Finland 64 E4

Kaka Turkmenistan *prev.* Kaakhka, *var.* Kaachka 102 C3

Kakhovs'ke Vodoskhovyshche *Reservoir* Ukraine 89 F3

Kalahari Desert *Desert* southern Africa 58 C3

Kalamariá Greece 84 B3

Kalámata Greece 85 B6

Kalāt Afghanistan 102 D5

Kalemie Zaire 57 E7

Kalgoorlie Australia 129 C6

Kaliningrad *External territory* Russian Federation 86 A4 94 A2

Kaliningrad Kaliningrad, Russian Federation *prev.* Königsberg 86 A4

Kalinkavichy Belorussia *Rus.* Kalinkovichi 87 D7

Kalinkovichi *see* Kalinkavichy

Kalisch *see* Kalisz

Kalispell Montana, USA 22 B1

Kalisz Poland *Ger.* Kalisch 78 C4

Kalmar Sweden 65 C7

Kalpeni Island *Island* India 116 C3

Kama *River* Russian Federation 90 D4

Kamchatka *Peninsula* Russian Federation 95 A3

Kamchiya *River* Bulgaria 84 E2

Kamina Zaire 57 D7

Kamishli *see* Al Qāmishlī

Kamloops Canada 17 E5

Kampala *Capital of* Uganda 55 B6

Kâmpóng Cham Cambodia 119 D6

Kâmpóng Chhnăng Cambodia 119 D5

Kâmpóng Saôm Cambodia 119 D6

Kâmpôt Cambodia 119 D6

Kampuchea *see* Cambodia

Kam"yanets'-Podil's'kyy Ukraine 88 C3

Kananga Zaire 57 D7

Kanazawa Japan 110 C4

Kandahār Afghanistan *var.* Qandahār 102 D5

Kandi Benin 53 F4

Kandla India 114 C4

Kandy Sri Lanka 117 E3

Kanestron, Ákra *Coastal feature* Greece 84 C4

Kangaatsiaq Greenland 62 B4

Kangaroo Island *Island* Australia 124 C4

Kangerlussuaq Greenland 62 B4

Kangertittivaq *Region* Greenland 62 D3

Kanggye North Korea 108 E4

Kanjiža Yugoslavia 80 D2

Kankan Guinea 52 D4

Kano Nigeria 53 G4

Kānpur India *prev.* Cawnpore 115 E3

Kansas *State* USA 22-23

Kansas City Kansas, USA 23 F4

Kansas City Missouri, USA 23 F4

Kansk Russian Federation 95 E4

Kao-hsiung Taiwan 109 D7

Kaolack Senegal 52 B3

Kapchagay Kazakhstan 94 C5

Kapfenberg Austria 75 E7

Kaposvár Hungary 79 C7

Kapsukas *see* Marijampolė

Kapuas *River* Indonesia 120 C4

Kara-Balta Kyrgyzstan 103 F2

Kara-Bogaz-Gol, Zaliv *Sea feature* Caspian Sea 102 A2

Karabük Turkey 96 C2

Karāchi Pakistan 114 B4

Karaganda Kazakhstan 94 C4

Karaj Iran 100 C3

Karakol Kyrgyzstan *prev.* Przheval'sk 103 G2

Kara Kum *Desert* Turkmenistan *see* Karakumy 92 C4

Karakumskiy Kanal *Canal* Turkmenistan *Turkm.* Garagum Kanaly 102 C3

Karakumy *Desert* Turkmenistan *Turkm.* Garagum, *var.* Qara Qum *Eng.* Kara Kum 102 C2

Karamay China 106 B2

Karasburg Namibia 58 C4

Kara Sea *see* Karskoye More

Karbalā' Iraq *var.* Kerbala 100 B3

Kardítsa Greece 84 B4

Kariba, Lake *Lake* Zambia/Zimbabwe 58 D2

Karkinits'ka Zatoka *Sea feature* Black Sea 89 E4

Karl-Marx-Stadt *see* Chemnitz

Karlovac Croatia 80 B3

Karlovy Vary Czech Republic *Ger.* Karlsbad 79 A5

Karlsbad *see* Karlovy Vary

Karlskrona Sweden 65 C7

Karlsruhe Germany 75 B6

Karlstad Sweden 65 B6

Karnātaka *State* India 116 D1

Kárpathos *Island* Greece 85 E7

Kars Turkey 97 F2

Karshi Uzbekistan *prev.* Bek-Budi, *Uzb.* Qarshi 102 D3

Karskoye More Arctic Ocean *Eng.* Kara Sea 13 E6 90 E2 94 D2

Kasai *River* Zaire 57 C6

Kasama Zambia 59 E1

Kaschau *see* Košice

Kāshān Iran 100 C3

Kashi China 106 A3

Kashmir *Disputed region* India/Pakistan 114 D1

Kasongo Zaire 57 E6

Kassa *see* Košice

Kassala Sudan 54 C4

Kassel Germany 74 B4
Kastamonu Turkey 96 C2
Kateríni Greece 84 B4
Katha Burma 118 B2
Katherine Australia 128 D2
Kathmandu *Capital of* Nepal
115 F3
Katsina Nigeria 53 G3
Kaue *see* Kaunas
Kauai *Island* USA
Kaunas Lithuania *Ger.* Kauen,
Pol. Kowno, *Rus.* Kovno 86 B4
Kavadarci Macedonia 80 E5
Kavála Greece 84 C3
Kavaratti Island *Island* India
116 C3
Kawasaki Japan 111 D5
Kayes Mali 52 C3
Kayseri Turkey 96 D3
Kazakhskiy Melkosopochnik
see Kazakh Upland
Kazakhstan *Country* C Asia 94
Kazakh Upland *Upland*
Kazakhstan *var.* Kazakhskiy
Melkosopochnik 92 D3
Kazan' Russian Federation 91
C5 94 B3
Kazandzhik *see* Gazandzhyk
Kazanlŭk Bulgaria 84 D2
Kazan *Island* Greece 85 C6
Kecskemét Hungary 79 D7
Kėdainiai Lithuania 86 B4
Keetmanshoop Namibia 58 C4
Kefallonía *Island* Greece
Eng. Cephalonia 85 A5
Keith Australia 130 B4
Kelang Malaysia 120 B3
Kelmė Lithuania 86 B4
Kelowna Canada 17 E5
Kemerovo Russian Federation
94 D4
Kemi Finland 64 D4
Kemi *River* Finland 64 D3
Kemijärvi Finland 64 D3
Kendari Indonesia 121 E4
Kenema Sierra Leone 52 C4
Këneurgench Turkmenistan
prev. Kunya-Urgench,
Turkm. Köneürgench 102 C2
Kénitra Morocco 50 C2
Kennewick Washington, USA
24 C2

Kenora Canada 18 A3
Kentucky *State* USA 20 C5
Kenya *Country* E Africa 55
Kenya, Mount *see* Kirinyaga
Kerala *State* India 116 D3
Kerbala *see* Karbalā'
Kerch Ukraine 89 G4
Kerguelen Islands *Island group*
Indian Ocean 113 C6
Kerguelen Plateau *Undersea
feature* Indian Ocean 113 C7
Kerki Turkmenistan 102 D3
Kérkira *see* Kérkyra
Kérkyra Greece 84 A4
Kérkyra *Island* Greece
prev. Kérkira, *Eng.* Corfu
84 A4
Kermadec Islands *Island group*
Pacific Ocean 125 F3
Kermadec Trench *Undersea
feature* Pacific Ocean 122 D4
Kermān Iran *var.* Kirman
100 D4
Kermānshāh *see* Bākhtarān
Kerora Eritrea 54 C3
Kerulen *River* China/Mongolia
107 E2
Ketchikan Alaska, USA 16 D4
Key West Florida, USA 29 E5
Khabarovsk Russian Federation
95 G4
Khanka, Lake *Lake*
China/Russian Federation
108 E3
Khankendy *see* Xankändi
Kharkiv Ukraine
Rus. Khar'kov 89 G2
Khartoum *Capital of* Sudan
var. Al Khurṭūm 54 B4
Khartoum North Sudan 54 B4
Khāsh Iran 100 E4
Khaskovo Bulgaria 84 D2
Khaydarkan Kyrgyzstan
var. Khaydarkan, Hajdarken
103 E2
Khaydarken *see* Khaydarkan
Kherson Ukraine 89 E4
Khíos *see* Chíos
Khmel 'nyts'kyy Ukraine 88 C2
Khodzhent *see* Khudzhand
Khojend *see* Khudzhand
Khokand *see* Kokand
Kholm Afghanistan 103 E3

Khon Kaen Thailand 118 C4
Khorog Tajikistan *var.* Horog
103 F3
Khorramshahr Iran
var. Khūnīnshahr 100 C4
Khouribga Morocco 50 C2
Khudzhand Tajikistan
prev. Leninabad, Khodzhent,
Khojend 103 E2
Khulna Bangladesh 115 G4
Khūnīnshahr *see* Khorramshahr
Khvoy Iran 100 B2
Kičevo Macedonia 81 D5
Kiel Germany 74 B2
Kielce Poland 78 D4
Kiev *Capital of* Ukraine
Ukr. Kyyiv 89 E2
Kiffa Mauritania 52 C3
Kigali *Capital of* Rwanda 55 B6
Kigoma Tanzania 55 B7
Kikládhes *see* Kyklades
Kikwit Zaire 57 C7
Kilimanjaro *Peak* Tanzania
49 D5
Kilkís Greece 84 B3
Killarney Ireland 69 A6
Kimberley South Africa 58 D4
Kimberley Plateau *Upland*
Australia 128 C3
Kindia Guinea 52 C4
Kindu Zaire 57 D6
King Island *Island* Australia
130 B4
Kingissepp *see* Kuressaare
Kingman Reef *External territory*
USA, Pacific Ocean 127 G2
Kingston Canada 18 C5
Kingston *Capital of* Jamaica
34 C3
Kingston upon Hull England,
UK *var.* Hull 69 D5
Kingstown St Vincent & The
Grenadines 34 G4
King William Island *Island*
Canada 17 F3
Kinneret, Yam *see* Tiberius, Lake
Kinshasa *Capital of* Zaire
prev. Léopoldville 57 B6
Kirghizia *see* Kyrgyzstan
Kirghiz Steppe *Plain*
Kazakhstan 95 B4
Kiribati *Country* Pacific
Ocean 122

Kirinyaga *Peak* Kenya
  var. Mount Kenya 49 D5
Kiritimati *Island* Kiribati
  var. Christmas Island 127 G2
Kirkenes Norway 64 E2
Kirklareli Turkey 96 A2
Kirkpatrick, Mount *Peak*
  Antarctica 132 D4
Kirksville Missouri, USA 23 G4
Kirkūk Iraq 100 B3
Kirkwall Scotland, UK 68 C2
Kirman *see* Kermān
Kirov Russian Federation 90 C4
  94 B3
Kirovabad *see* Gäncä
Kirovakan *see* Vanadzor
Kirovohrad Ukraine 89 E8
Kiruna Sweden 64 C3
Kisangani Zaire
  prev. Stanleyville 57 D5
Kishinev *see* Chişinău
Kiska Island *Island* Alaska, USA
  16 A2
Kismaayo Somalia 55 D6
Kisumu Kenya 55 C6
Kitakyūshū Japan 111 A5
Kitami Japan 110 D2
Kitchener Canada 18 C5
Kitwe Zambia 58 D2
Kivu, Lake *Lake* Rwanda/Zaire
  55 B6 57 E6
Kızıl Irmak *River* Turkey 96 C2
Kizil Kum *see* Kyzyl Kum
Kizyl-Arvat *see* Gyzylarbat
Kjølen Mountains *Mountain
  range* Sweden *see* Kölen
  60 D2
Kladno Czech Republic 79 A5
Klagenfurt Austria 75 D7
Klaipėda Lithuania *Ger.* Memel
  86 B4
Klamath Falls Oregon, USA
  24 B4
Ključ Bosnia & Herzegovina
  80 B3
Knin Croatia 80 B4
Knittelfeld Austria 75 D7
Knoxville Tennessee, USA 29 E1
Knud Rasmussen Land *Region*
  Greenland 62 B2
Kōbe Japan 111 C5
Koblenz Germany 75 A5
Kobryn Belorussia 87 B6

Kocaeli *see* İzmit
Kočani Macedonia 81 E5
Kōchi Japan 111 B6
Kodiak Alaska, USA 16 C3
Kodiak Island *Island* Alaska,
  USA 16 C3
Kohīma India 115 H3
Kohtla-Järve Estonia 86 D2
Kokand Uzbekistan
  var. Khokand, *Uzb.* Qŭqon
  103 E2
Kokchetav Kazakhstan 94 C4
Kokkola Finland 64 D4
Koko Nor *see* Qinghai Hu
Kokshaal-Tau *Mountain range*
  Kyrgyzstan 103 G2
Kolda Senegal 52 B3
Kölen *see* Kjølen Mountains
Kolguyev, Ostrov *Island* Russian
  Federation 90 D2
Kolhumadulu Atoll *Island*
  Maldives 116 C5
Kolka Latvia 86 B2
Köln Germany *Eng.* Cologne
  75 A5
Kol'skiy Poluostrov *Peninsula*
  Russian Federation *Eng.* Kola
  Peninsula 61 F1 90 C2
Kolwezi Zaire 57 D8
Kolyma Range *Mountain range*
  Russian Federation 93 G2
Komárno Slovakia *Ger.* Komorn,
  Hung. Komárom 79 C6
Komárom *see* Komárno
Kommunizma, Pik *see*
  Communism Peak
Komoé *River* Ivory Coast
  53 E4
Komorn *see* Komárno
Komotau *see* Chomutov
Komotiní Greece 84 D3
Komsomol'sk Turkmenistan
  102 D3
Komsomol'sk-na-Amure
  Russian Federation 95 G4
Kondoz *see* Kunduz
Kondūz *see* Kunduz
Köneürgench *see* Këneurgench
Kong Christian IX Land *Region*
  Greenland 62 D3
Kong Christian X Land *Region*
  Greenland 62 D3

Kong Frederik VI Kyst *Region*
  Greenland 62 C4
Kong Frederik VIII Land *Region*
  Greenland 62 D2
Kong Frederik IX Land *Region*
  Greenland 62 C4
Kongsvinger Norway 65 B6
Konia *see* Konya
Königgrätz *see* Hradec Králové
Königsberg *see* Kaliningrad
Konispol Albania 81 D7
Konjic Bosnia & Herzegovina
  80 C4
Konya Turkey *prev.* Konia 96 C4
Kopaonik *Mountains* Yugoslavia
  81 D4
Koper Slovenia 80 A3
Koprivnica Croatia 80 B2
Korçë Albania 81 D6
Korčula *Island* Croatia 80 B4
Korea Strait *Sea feature*
  Japan/South Korea 108-109 E5
Korhogo Ivory Coast 52 D4
Korinthiakós Kólpos *Sea feature*
  Greece *Eng.* Gulf of Corinth
  85 B5
Kórinthos Greece *Eng.* Corinth
  85 B5
Kōriyama Japan 111 D4
Korla China 106 B3
Koror *Capital of* Palau 126 A1
Körös *River* Hungary 79 D7
Korosten' Ukraine 88 D1
Kortrijk Belgium 67 A6
Kos *Island* Greece 85 E6
Kosciusko, Mount *Peak*
  Australia 124 C4
Košice Slovakia *Ger.* Kaschau,
  Hung. Kassa 79 D6
Köslin *see* Koszalin
Kosovo *Province* Yugoslavia
  81 D5
Kosovska Mitrovica Yugoslavia
  80 D4
Kosrae *Island* Micronesia
  126 C2
Koszalin Poland *Ger.* Köslin
  78 B2
Kota India 114 D4
Kota Bharu Malaysia 120 B3
Kota Kinabalu Malaysia 120 D3
Kotka Finland 65 E5
Kotlas NW Russia 90 C4

Kotto *River* C Africa 56 D4
Koudougou Burkina 53 E4
Kourou French Guiana 39 H2
Kousséri Cameroon 56 B3
Kouvola Finland 65 E5
Kovel' Ukraine 88 C1
Kovno *see* Kaunas
Kowno *see* Kaunas
Kozáni Greece 84 B4
Kozhikode *see* Calicut
Kra, Isthmus of *Coastal feature* Burma/Thailand 119 B6
Kragujevac Yugoslavia 80 D4
Krakatau *Peak* Indonesia 104 D5
Krakau *see* Kraków
Kraków Poland *Eng.* Cracow, *Ger.* Krakau 79 D5
Kraljevo Yugoslavia 80 D4
Kranj Slovenia 80 A2
Krasnodar Russian Federation 91 A6
Krasnovodsk *see* Turkmenbashy
Krasnoyarsk Russian Federation 94 D4
Krasnyy Luch Ukraine 89 G5
Kremenchuk Ukraine 89 F2
Kremenchuts'ke Vodoskhovyshche *Reservoir* Ukraine 89 E2
Krems an der Donau Austria 75 E6
Kretinga Lithuania *Ger.* Krottingen 86 B3
Kribi Cameroon 57 B5
Krichev *see* Krychaw
Krishna *River* India 116 C1
Kristiansand Norway 65 A6
Kristianstad Sweden 65 B7
Kríti *Island* Greece *Eng.* Crete 85 C7
Kritikó Pélagos *see* Crete, Sea of
Krivoy Rog *see* Kryvyy Rih
Krk *Island* Croatia 80 A3
Kroonstad South Africa 58 D4
Krottingen *see* Kretinga
Krung Thep *see* Bangkok
Kruševac Yugoslavia 81 D4
Krychaw Belorussia *Rus.* Krichev 87 E6
Krym *see* Crimea
Kryvyy Rih Ukraine *Rus.* Krivoy Rog 89 E3

Kuala Lumpur *Capital of* Malaysia 120 B3
Kuala Terengganu Malaysia 120 B3
Kuantan Malaysia 120 B3
Kuba *see* Quba
Kuching Malaysia 120 C3
Kuçovë Albania *prev.* Qyteti Stalin 81 D6
Kuito Angola 58 C2
Kuldīga Latvia *Ger.* Goldingen 86 B3
Kullorsuaq Greenland 62 B3
Kulyab SW Tajikistan 103 E3
Kum *see* Qom
Kuma *River* Russian Federation 91 B7
Kumamoto Japan 111 A6
Kumanovo Macedonia 81 E5
Kumasi Ghana 53 E5
Kumayri *see* Gyumri 97 F2
Kumbo Cameroon 56 B4
Kumon Range *Mountain range* Burma 118 B1
Kunashir *Island* Japan/Russian Federation (disputed) 110 E1
Kunduz Afghanistan *var.* Kondūz, Qondūz, Kondoz 103 E3
Kunja-Urgenč *see* Këneurgench
Kunlun Mountains *see* Kunlun Shan
Kunlun Shan *Mountain range* China *Eng.* Kunlun Mountains 104 C2 106 B4
Kunming China 109 A6
Kununurra Australia 128 D3
Kupang Indonesia 120 E5
Kür *see* Kura
Kura *River* Azerbaijan/Georgia *Az.* Kür 96 G2
Kurashiki Japan 111 B5
Küre Dağları *Mountains* Turkey 96 C2
Kuressaare Estonia *prev.* Kingissepp, *Ger.* Arensburg 86 C2
Kurgan-Tyube Tajikistan 103 E3
Kurile Islands *Islands* Pacific Ocean 105 F1
Kurile Trench *Undersea feature* Pacific Ocean 122 C2
Kurmuk Sudan 54 C4

Kurnool India 116 D2
Kuršėnai Lithuania 86 B4
Kushiro Japan 110 E2
Kushka *see* Gushgy
Kustanay Kazakhstan 94 C4
Kütahya Turkey *prev.* Kutaiah 96 B3
Kutaiah *see* Kütahya
K'ut'aisi Georgia 97 F2
Kutch, Rann of *see* Kachch, Rann of
Kuujjuaq Canada 19 E2
Kuujjuarapik Canada 18 D2
Kuusamo Finland 64 E3
Kuwait *Country* SW Asia 100 C4
Kuwait City *Capital of* Kuwait 100 C4
Kuytun China 106 B3
Kwangju South Korea 109 E5
Kwango *River* Zaire 57 C7
Kykládes *Island group* Greece *prev.* Kikládhes, *Eng.* Cyclades 85 D6
Kyrenia *see* Girne
Kyrgyzstan *Country* C Asia *var.* Kirghizia 103
Kýthira *Island* Greece 85 B6
Kyushu-Palau Ridge *Undersea feature* Pacific Ocean 111 B7 121 G1
Kyushu *Island* Japan 111 B6
Kyōto Japan 111 C5
Kyyiv *see* Kiev
Kyzyl Kum *Desert* Kazakhstan/Uzbekistan *var.* Kizil Kum, *Uzb.* Qizilqum 92 C3
Kyzl-Orda Kazakhstan 94 B5

L

Laâyoune Western Sahara 50 B3
Labé Guinea 52 C4
Laborca *see* Laborec
Laborec *River* Slovakia *Hung.* Laborca 79 E5
Labrador *Region* Canada 19 F2
Labrador Basin *Undersea feature* Atlantic Ocean 15 G2 19 G1
Labrador City Canada 19 E3
Labrador Sea Atlantic Ocean 62 B5

Lethbridge Canada 17 F5
Leti, Kepulauan *Island group*
Indonesia 121 F5
Leuven Belgium 67 C6
Leverkusen Germany 75 A5
Levkás *see* Lefkáda
Lewis *Island* Scotland, UK 68 B2
Lewiston Idaho, USA 24 C2
Lewiston Maine, USA 21 G2
Lexington Kentucky, USA 20 C5
Leyte *Island* Philippines 121 E2
Lezhë Albania 81 D5
Lhasa China 106 C5
Liangyungang China 109 D5
Liaoyuan China 108 D3
Libau *see* Liepāja
Liberec Czech Republic
Ger. Reichenberg 78 B4
Liberia *Country* W Africa 52
Liberia Costa Rica 32 D4
Libreville *Capital of* Gabon
57 A5
Libya *Country* N Africa 51
Libyan Desert *Desert* N Africa
48 C3
Liechtenstein *Country* C Europe
75 B7
Liège Belgium 67 D6
Liegnitz *see* Legnica
Lienz Austria 75 D7
Liepāja Latvia *Ger.* Libau 86 B3
Liffey *River* Ireland 69 B5
Ligurian Sea Mediterranean Sea
71 E6
Likasi Zaire 57 E8
Lille France 70 C2
Lillehammer Norway 65 B5
Lilongwe *Capital of* Malawi
59 E2
Lima *Capital of* Peru 40 B4
Lima Ohio, USA 20 C4
Limassol Cyprus *var.* Lemesos
96 C5
Limerick Ireland 69 A6
Límnos *Island* Greece
var. Lemnos 84 C4
Limoges France 70 C5
Limón Costa Rica 33 E4
Limpopo *River* southern Africa
58 D3
Linares Chile 44 B4
Linares Spain 73 E4

Lincoln England, UK 69 D5
Lincoln Nebraska, USA 23 F4
Lincoln Sea Arctic Ocean
62 B1
Linden Guyana 39 G2
Lindi *River* Zaire 55 C8
Line Islands *Island group*
Kiribati 127 H3
Lingga, Kepulauan *Island group*
Indonesia 120 B4
Linköping Sweden 65 C6
Linosa *Island* Italy 77 C8
Linz Austria 75 D6
Lion, Golfe du *Sea feature*
Mediterranean Sea 82 C2
Lipari *Island* Italy 77 D6
Lipari Islands *see* Isole Eolie
Lira Uganda 55 B6
Lisbon *Capital of* Portugal
Port. Lisboa 72 B4
Litang China 109 A5
Litani *River* SW Asia 89 B4
Lithuania *Country* E Europe
86-87
Little Andaman *Island* India
117 G2
Little Minch *Sea feature*
Scotland, UK 68 B3
Little Rock Arkansas, USA
28 B2
Liuzhou China 109 B7
Liverpool England, UK 69 D5
Livingston, Lake *Lake* Texas,
USA 27 H3
Livingstone Zambia 58 D3
Livno Bosnia & Herzegovina
80 B4
Livorno Italy 76 B3
Ljubljana *Capital of* Slovenia
80 A2
Ljusnan *River* Sweden 65 B5
Llanos *Region*
Colombia/Venezuela 39 E2
Lleida Spain *Cast.* Lérida 73 F2
Lobatse Botswana 58 D4
Lobito Angola 58 B2
Locarno Switzerland 75 B8
Lodja Zaire 57 D6
Łódź Poland *Rus.* Lodz 78 D4
Lofoten *Island group* Norway
64 B3
Logan, Mount *Peak* Canada
14 C2

Logroño Spain 73 E2
Loire *River* France 70 B4
Loja Ecuador 38 A5
Lokitaung Kenya 55 C5
Loksa Estonia *Ger.* Loxa 86 D2
Lombok *Island* Indonesia
120 D5
Lomé *Capital of* Togo 53 F5
Lomond, Loch *Lake* Scotland,
UK 68 C4
Lomonosov Ridge *Undersea*
feature Arctic Ocean
var. Harris Ridge 12 D4
London Canada 18 C5
London *Capital of* UK 69 E6
Londonderry Northern Ireland,
UK 68 B4
Londonderry, Cape *Coastal*
feature Australia 124 B2
128 C2
Londrina Brazil 42 D2
Long Beach California, USA
25 C8
Long Island *Island* Bahamas
34 D2
Long Island *Island* NE USA
21 G3
Longreach Australia 126 B5
Longview Texas, USA 27 G3
Longview Washington, USA
24 B2
Longyearbyen Svalbard 63 G2
Lop Nur *Lake* China 106 C3
Lorca Spain 73 F4
Lord Howe Rise *Undersea feature*
Pacific Ocean 122 C4
Lorient France 70 A3
Los Alamos New Mexico, USA
26 D2
Los Angeles California, USA
25 C8
Loslau *see* Wodzisław Śląski
Los Mochis Mexico 30 C3
Losonc *see* Lučenec
Losontz *see* Lučenec
Lot *River* France 71 B5
Louangphrabang Laos 118 C3
Loubomo Congo 57 B6
Louisiana *State* USA 28 B3
Louisville Kentucky, USA 20 C5
Lovech Bulgaria 84 C2
Lower California *see* Baja
California

Loxa *see* Loksa
Loyauté, Îles *Island group* New
　Caledonia 126 D5
Loznica Yugoslavia 80 C3
Luanda *Capital of* Angola 58 B1
Luanshya Zambia 58 D2
Lubānas Ezers *Lake* Latvia
　86 D4
Lubango Angola 58 B2
Lubbock Texas, USA 27 E2
Lübeck Germany 74 C3
Lublin Poland *Rus.* Lyublin
　78 E4
Lubny Ukraine 89 F2
Lubumbashi Zaire 57 E8
Lucapa Angola 58 C1
Lucena Philippines 120 E1
Lučenec Slovakia *Hung.* Losonc,
　Ger. Losontz 79 D6
Lucerne *see* Luzern
Lucknow India 115 E3
Lüderitz Namibia 58 B4
Ludhiāna India 114 D2
Lugano Switzerland 75 B8
Lugo Spain 72 C1
Luhans'k Ukraine 89 H3
Luleå Sweden 64 D4
Lumsden New Zealand 131 F5
Luninyets Belorussia 97 C6
Lusaka *Capital of* Zambia 58 D2
Lushnjë Albania 81 D6
Lūt, Baḥrat *see* Dead Sea
Luts'k Ukraine 88 C1
Lutzow-Holm Bay *Sea feature*
　Antarctica 133 F1
Luxembourg *Country* W Europe
　67 D8
Luxembourg *Capital of*
　Luxembourg 67 D8
Luxor Egypt 54 B2
Luzern Switzerland *Fr.* Lucerne
　75 B7
Luzon *Island* Philippines 121 E1
Luzon Strait *Sea feature*
　Philippines/Taiwan 105 E3
L'viv Ukraine *Rus.* L'vov 88 B2
L'vov *see* L'viv
Lyepyel' Belorussia *Rus.* Lepel'
　87 D5
Lyon France 71 D5
Lyublin *see* Lublin

M

Ma'ān Jordan 99 B6
Maas *River* W Europe
　var. Meuse 66 D4
Maastricht Netherlands 67 D6
Macao *External territory*
　Portugal, E Asia *var.* Macau
　109 C7
Macapá Brazil 41 F1
Macau *see* Macao
Macdonald Islands *Islands*
　Indian Ocean 113 B7
Macdonnell Ranges *Mountains*
　Australia 128 D4
Macedonia *Country* SE Europe
　officially Former Yugoslav
　Republic of Macedonia,
　abbrev. FYR Macedonia 81
Maceió Brazil 41 H3
Machakos Kenya 55 C6
Machala Ecuador 38 A5
Mackay Australia 126 B5
　130 C1
Mackay, Lake *Lake* Australia
　128 D4
Mackenzie *River* Canada 17 E4
Mackenzie Bay *Sea feature*
　Atlantic Ocean 133 G2
Mâcon France 70 D5
Macon Georgia, USA 29 E2
Madagascar *Country* Indian
　Ocean 59
Madagascar Basin *Undersea
　feature* Indian Ocean 113 B5
Madagascar Ridge *Undersea
　feature* Indian Ocean 113 A5
Madang Papua New Guinea
　126 B3
Madeira *River* Bolivia/Brazil
　40 D2
Madeira *Island group* Portugal
　50 A2
Madhya Pradesh *State* India
　115 E4
Madison Wisconsin, USA
　20 B3
Madona Latvia *Ger.* Modohn
　86 D3
Madras India 117 E2
Madre de Dios *River*
　Bolivia/Peru 40 C3
Madrid *Capital of* Spain 73 E3
Madurai India 116 D3

Magadan Russian Federation
　95 G3
Magallanes *see* Punta Arenas
Magallanes, Estrecho de *see*
　Magellan, Strait of
Magdalena *River* Colombia
　38 B2
Magdeburg Germany 74 C4
Magellan, Strait of *Sea feature*
　S South America *Sp.* Estrecho
　de Magallanes 37 B7
Maggiore, Lake *Lake*
　Italy/Switzerland 75 B8
Mahajanga Madagascar
　59 G2
Mahalapye Botswana 58 D3
Mahanādi *River* India 115 F5
Mahārāshtra *State* India
　114 D5
Mahé *Island* Seychelles 59 H1
Mahilyow Belorussia
　Rus. Mogilëv 87 E6
Mährisch-Ostrau *see* Ostrava
Maicao Colombia 38 C1
Maiduguri Nigeria 53 H4
Maimana *see* Meymaneh
Maine *State* USA 21 G1
Mainz Germany 75 B5
Maiquetía Venezuela 38 D1
Maíz, Islas del *Islands*
　Nicaragua 33 E3 34 B5
Majorca *see* Mallorca
Majuro *Island* Marshall Islands
　126 D1
Makarska Croatia 80 B4
Makeni Sierra Leone 52 C4
Makeyevka *see* Makiyivka
Makgadikgadi *Salt pan*
　Botswana 58 D3
Makhachkala Russian
　Federation 91 B7 94 A4
Makiyivka Ukraine
　Rus. Makeyevka 89 G5
Makkah Saudi Arabia
　Eng. Mecca 101 A5
Makkovik Canada 19 G2
Makurdi Nigeria 53 G4
Malabo *Capital of* Equatorial
　Guinea 57 A5
Malacca *see* Melaka
Malacca, Strait of *Sea feature*
　Indonesia/ Malaysia 104 C4
　119 C8

Maladzyechna Belorussia
Rus. Molodechno,
Pol. Molodeczno 87 C5

Málaga Spain 72 D5

Malakal Sudan 55 B5

Malang Indonesia 120 D5

Malanje Angola 58 B1

Malatya Turkey 97 E3

Malawi *Country* southern
Africa 59

Malay Peninsula *Peninsula*
Malaysia/Thailand 119 D8

Malaysia *Country* Asia 120

Maldive Ridge *Undersea feature*
Indian Ocean 112 C4

Maldives *Country* Indian Ocean
116

Male' *Capital of* Maldives
116 C4

Mali *Country* W Africa 53

Malindi Kenya 55 C7

Mallorca Spain
Eng. Majorca 73 H3

Malmö Sweden 65 B5

Malta *Country* Mediterranean
Sea 77 C8

Malta Montana, USA 22 C1

Malta Channel *Sea feature*
Mediterranean Sea 77 C7

Maluku *Island group* Indonesia
var. Moluccas 105 E4 121 F4

Maluku, Laut Pacific Ocean
Eng. Molucca Sea 121 F4

Māmallapuram India 117 E2

Mamberamo *River* Indonesia
121 H4

Mamoudzou *Capital of* Mayotte
59 G2

Man Ivory Coast 52 D4

Man, Isle of *Island* UK 69 C5

Manado Indonesia 120 F3

Managua *Capital of* Nicaragua
32 D3

Manama *Capital of* Bahrain
Ar. Al Manāmah 101 C5

Mananjary Madagascar 59 G3

Manaus Brazil 40 D2

Manchester England, UK 69 D5

Manchester New Hampshire,
USA 21 G2

Manchuria *Region* China 108 D3

Manchurian Plain *Plain* E Asia
105 E1

Mandalay Burma 118 B3

Mangalia Romania 88 D5

Mangalore India 116 C2

Manguéni, Plateau du *Upland*
Niger 53 H2

Manicouagan, Réservoir
Reservoir Canada 19 E3

Manila *Capital of* Philippines
120 E1

Manisa Turkey *prev.* Saruhan
96 A3

Manitoba *Province* Canada
17 G4

Manizales Colombia 38 B3

Manjimup Australia 129 B6

Manlitsoq Greenland 62 B4

Mannar Sri Lanka 117 E3

Mannar, Gulf of *Sea feature*
Indian Ocean 116 D3

Mannheim Germany 75 B5

Mannu *River* Italy 77 A5

Manono Zaire 57 E7

Mansel Island *Island* Canada
18 C1

Manta Ecuador 38 A4

Mantes-la-Jolie France 70 C3

Mantova Italy *Eng.* Mantua
76 B2

Mantua *see* Mantova

Manzhouli China 107 F1

Mao Chad 56 B3

Maoke, Pegunungan *Mountains*
Indonesia 121 H4

Maputo *Capital of* Mozambique
59 E4

Mar, Serra do *Mountains* Brazil
36 D4

Maracaibo Venezuela 38 C1

Maracaibo, Lago de *Inlet*
Venezuela 38 C1

Maracay Venezuela 38 D1

Maradi Niger 53 G3

Marajó, Ilha de *Island* Brazil
40 E2

Marañón *River* Peru 40 B2

Maraş *see* Kahramanmaraş

Marash *see* Kahramanmaraş

Marbella Spain 72 D5

Mar Chiquita, Laguna *Salt lake*
Argentina 44 D3

Mardān Pakistan 114 C1

Mar del Plata Argentina 45 D5

Mardin Turkey 97 E4

Margarita, Isla de *Island*
Venezuela 35 F3 39 E1

Mārgow, Dasht-e- *Desert*
Afghanistan 102 C5

Mariana Trench *Undersea feature*
Pacific Ocean 122 C2

Marías, Islas *Islands* Mexico
30 C4

Maribor Slovenia 80 B2

Marie Byrd Land *Region*
Antarctica 132 C3

Mariehamn Finland 65 D6

Marijampolė Lithuania
prev. Kapsukas 86 B4

Marília Brazil 41 F5 42 D2

Maringá Brazil 42 D2

Marion, Lake Lake South
Carolina, USA 29 F2

Mariscal Estigarribia Paraguay
42 B2

Maritsa *River* SE Europe 84 D3

Mariupol' Ukraine
prev. Shdanov 89 G4

Marka Somalia 55 D6

Markham, Mount *Peak*
Antarctica 132 D4

Marmara, Sea of *see* Marmara
Denizi

Marmara Denizi Turkey
Eng. Sea of Marmara 96 B2

Marne *River* France 70 D3

Maroua Cameroon 56 B3

Marowijne *River* French
Guiana/Surinam 39 H3

Marquesas Islands *Island group*
French Polynesia *Fr.* Îles
Marquises 125 H2

Marquette Michigan, USA 20 B1

Marquisas, Îles *see* Marquesas
Islands

Marrakech Morocco
Eng. Marrakesh 50 B2

Marsala Italy 77 C7

Marseille France 71 D6

Marshall Islands *Country* Pacific
Ocean 126-127

Marsh Island *Island* Louisiana,
USA 29 B4

Martin Slovakia *prev.* Turčiansky
Svätý Martin,
Ger. Sankt Martin,
Hung. Turócszentmárton
79 C5

Martinique *External territory*
France, West Indies 35

Mary Turkmenistan *prev.* Merv 102 C3
Maryland *State* USA 21 F4
Mascarene Islands *Island group* Indian Ocean 59 H3
Mascarene Plateau *Undersea feature* Indian Ocean 113 B5
Maseru *Capital of* Lesotho 58 D4
Mashhad Iran *var.* Meshed 100 E3
Masindi Uganda 55 B6
Mason City Iowa, USA 23 F3
Masqaṭ *see* Muscat
Massachusetts *State* USA 21 G3
Massawa Eritrea 54 C4
Massif Central *Upland* France 71 C5
Massoukou Gabon 57 B6
Masterton New Zealand 131 G3
Matadi Zaire 57 B7
Matagalpa Nicaragua 32 D3
Matamoros Mexico 31 E2
Matanzas Cuba 34 B2
Matara Sri Lanka 117 E4
Mataró Spain 73 G2
Mato Grosso, Planalto de *Upland* Brazil 41 E3
Matosinhos Portugal 72 C2
Matrûh Egypt 54 B1
Matsue Japan 111 B5
Matsuyama Japan 111 B5
Maturín Venezuela 39 E1
Maun Botswana 58 D3
Mauritania *Country* W Africa 52
Mauritius *Country* Indian Ocean 59 H3
Mayaguana *Island* Bahamas 34 D2
Mayotte *External territory* France, Indian Ocean 59 G2
Mayyit, Al Baḥr al *see* Dead Sea
Mazār-e Sharîf Afghanistan 102 D3
Mazatenango Guatemala 32 B2
Mazatlán Mexico 30 C3
Mažeikiai Lithuania 86 B3
Mazury *Region* Poland 78 D3
Mazyr Belorussia *Rus.* Mozyr' 87 D7
Mbabane *Capital of* Swaziland 59 E4
Mbala Zambia 59 E1

Mbale Uganda 55 C6
Mbandaka Zaire 57 C5
Mbeya Tanzania 55 B8
Mbuji-Mayi Zaire 57 D7
McKinley, Mount *see* Denali
McMurdo Sound *Sea feature* Antarctica 133 E5
Mead, Lake *Lake* SW USA 25 D7 26 A1
Mecca *see* Makkah
Mechelen Belgium 67 C5
Medan Indonesia 120 A3
Medellín Colombia 38 B2
Médenine Tunisia 51 F2
Medford Oregon, USA 24 B4
Medina *see* Al Madînah
Mediterranean Sea *Atlantic Ocean* 82-83
Meekatharra Australia 129 B5
Meerut India 114 D3
Mek'elê Ethiopia 54 C4
Meknès Morocco 50 C2
Mekong *River* SE Asia 104 D3
Mekong Delta *Wetlands* Vietnam 119 E6
Melaka Malaysia *prev.* Malacca 120 B3
Melanesia *Region* Pacific Ocean 124-125 126-127
Melbourne Australia 130 B4
Melbourne Florida, USA 29 F5
Melilla *External territory* Spain, N Africa 50 C1
Melitopol' Ukraine 89 F4
Melo Uruguay 42 C4
Melville Island *Island* Australia 128 D2
Melville Island *Island* Canada 17 E2
Memel *see* Klaipėda
Memel *see* Neman
Memphis Tennessee, USA 28 C2
Mende France 71 C6
Mendi Papua New Guinea 126 B3
Mendoza Argentina 44 B4
Menongue Angola 58 C2
Menorca *Island* Spain *Eng.* Minorca 73 H3
Mentawai, Kepulauan *Island group* Indonesia 120 A4
Meppel Netherlands 66 D2

Merced California, USA 25 B6
Mercedario *Peak* Argentina 37 B5
Mercedes Argentina 44 C4
Mercedes Uruguay 42 B3
Mergui Burma 119 B5
Mergui Archipelago *Island chain* Burma 119 B6
Mérida Mexico 31 H3
Mérida Spain 72 D4
Mérida Venezuela 38 C2
Meridian Mississippi, USA 28 C3
Merredin Australia 129 B6
Mersin Turkey *var.* İçel 96 C4
Meru Kenya 55 C5
Merv *see* Mary
Mesa Arizona, USA 26 B2
Meshed *see* Mashhad
Messina Italy 77 D6
Messina, Stretto di *Sea feature* Ionian Sea / Tyrrhenian Sea 77 D7
Mesters Vig Greenland 62 D3
Mestre Italy 76 C2
Meta *River* Colombia / Venezuela 38 C2
Metković Croatia 80 C4
Metz France 70 D3
Meuse *River* W Europe *var.* Maas 70 D3
Mexicali Mexico 30 A1
Mexicana, Altiplanicie *see* Mexico, Plateau of
Mexico *Country* North America 30-31
México, Golfo de *see* Mexico, Gulf of
Mexico, Gulf of *Sea feature* Atlantic Ocean / Caribbean Sea 46 A4
Mexico, Plateau of *Upland* Mexico *Sp.* Altiplanicie Mexicana 14 D4
Mexico City *Capital of* Mexico *Sp.* Ciudad de México 31 E4
Meymaneh Afghanistan *var.* Maimana 102 D4
Mezen' *River* Russian Federation 90 D3
Miami Florida, USA 29 F5
Michigan *State* USA 20 C2

Michigan, Lake *Lake* USA 20 C2

Micronesia *Country* Pacific Ocean 126

Micronesia *Region* Pacific Ocean 126-127

Mid Atlantic Ridge *Undersea feature* Atlantic Ocean 46 B4

Middelburg South Africa 58 D5

Middle America Trench *Undersea feature* Pacific Ocean 36 A1

Middle Andaman *Island* India 117 C2

Middlesbrough England, UK 69 D5

Mid-Indian Ridge *Undersea feature* Indian Ocean 113 C5

Midland Texas, USA 27 E2

Mikhaylovka Russian Federation 91 B6

Mikkeli Finland 65 E5

Míkonos *Island* Greece 85 D6

Milagro Ecuador 38 A4

Milan *see* Milano

Milano Italy *Eng.* Milan 76 B2

Mildura Australia 130 B3

Miles Australia 130 C2

Miles City Montana, USA 22 C2

Milford Haven Wales, UK 69 C6

Milford Sound New Zealand 131 E4

Mílos *Island* Greece 85 C6

Milparinka Australia 130 B2

Milwaukee Wisconsin, USA 20 B3

Minatitlán Mexico 31 G4

Mindanao *Island* Philippines 121 F2

Mindoro *Island* Philippines 121 E2

Mindoro Strait *Sea feature* South China Sea/Sulu Sea 121 E2

Mingäçevir Azerbaijan *Rus.* Mingechaur 97 G2

Mingechaur *see* Mingäçevir

Minho *River* Portugal/Spain *Sp.* Miño 72 C2

Minicoy Island *Island* India 116 C3

Minneapolis Minnesota, USA 23 F2

Minnesota *State* USA 23 F1

Miño *River* Portugal/Spain *Port.* Minho 72 C1

Minorca *see* Menorca

Minot North Dakota, USA 22 D1

Minsk *Capital of* Belorussia 87 C5

Minto, Lake *Lake* Canada 18 D2

Miranda de Ebro Spain 73 E2

Mirim, Lake *Lagoon* Brazil/Uruguay *var.* Mirim Lagoon 42 C5

Mirtóo Pelagos *Sea feature* Mediterranean Sea 85 C6

Miskitos Cayos *Islands* Nicaragua 33 E2

Miskolc Hungary 79 D6

Mişrātah Libya 51 F2

Mississippi *State* USA 28 C2

Mississippi *River* USA 15 E4

Mississippi Delta *Wetlands* USA 15 E4

Missoula Montana, USA 22 B2

Missouri *State* USA 23 G5

Missouri *River* USA 23 G4

Mistassini, Lake *Lake* Canada 18 D3

Mitau *see* Jelgava

Mitchell South Dakota, USA 23 E3

Mitilíni Greece 84 D4

Mito Japan 110 D4

Miyazaki Japan 111 B6

Mjosa *Lake* Norway 65 B5

Mljet *Island* Croatia 81 C5

Mmabatho South Africa 58 D4

Mo Norway 64 C3

Mobile Alabama, USA 28 C3

Moçambique Mozambique 59 F2

Mocímboa da Praia Mozambique 59 F2

Mocoa Colombia 38 B4

Mocuba Mozambique 59 F2

Modena Italy 76 B3

Modesto California, USA 25 B6

Mödling Austria 75 E6

Modohn *see* Madona

Modriča Bosnia & Herzegovina 80 C3

Mogadiscio *see* Mogadishu

Mogadishu *Capital of* Somalia *Som.* Muqdisho, *It.* Mogadiscio 55 D6

Mogilëv *see* Mahilyow

Mohéli *Island* Comoros 59 F2

Mohns Ridge *Undersea feature* Greenland Sea 63 F3

Mojave California, USA 25 C7

Mojave Desert *Desert* W USA 25 D7

Moldavia *Country* E Europe *var.* Moldova 88

Molde Norway 65 A5

Moldova *see* Moldavia

Molodechno *see* Maladzyechna

Molodeczno *see* Maladzyechna

Molotov *see* Perm'

Moluccas *see* Maluku

Molucca Sea *see* Maluku, Laut

Mombasa Kenya 55 C7

Monaco *Country* W Europe 71 E6

Monastir Tunisia 51 F1

Monclova Mexico 31 E2

Moncton Canada 19 F4

Mongo Chad 56 C3

Mongolia *Country* NE Asia 106-107

Monroe Louisiana, USA 28 B2

Monrovia *Capital of* Liberia 52 C5

Mons Belgium 67 B6

Montague Seamount *Undersea feature* Atlantic Ocean 43 H1

Montana *State* USA 22 C2

Montauban France 71 B6

Mont Blanc *Peak* France/Italy 60 D4

Mont-de-Marsan France 70 B6

Monte-Carlo Monaco 71 E6

Montecristi Dominican Republic 35 E3

Montego Bay Jamaica 34 C3

Montenegro *Republic* Yugoslavia 81 D5

Monterey California, USA 25 B6

Montería Colombia 38 B2

Montero Bolivia 40 D4

Monterrey Mexico 31 E2

Montes Claros Brazil 41 G4

Montevideo *Capital of* Uruguay 42 C5

Montgomery Alabama, USA 28 D3

Montpelier Vermont, USA 21 F2

Montpellier France 71 C6

Montréal Canada 19 E4
Montreux Switzerland 75 A5
Montserrat *External territory* UK, West Indies 35
Monument Valley *Valley* SW USA 26 C1
Monywa Burma 118 A3
Monza Italy 76 B2
Moora Australia 129 B6
Moorhead Minnesota, USA 23 E2
Moosonee Canada 18 C3
Mopti Mali 53 E3
Morava *River* C Europe 79 B6 80 E4
Moravská Ostrava *see* Ostrava
Morawhanna Guyana 39 F2
Moray Firth *Inlet* Scotland, UK 68 C3
Moree Australia 130 C2
Morehead City North Carolina, USA 29 G2
Morelia Mexico 31 E4
Morena, Sierra *Mountain range* Spain 72 D4
Morghāb *River* Afghanistan/Turkmenistan 102 D4
Morioka Japan 110 D3
Morocco *Country* N Africa 50
Morogoro Tanzania 55 C7
Morondava Madagascar 59 F3
Moroni *Capital of* Comoros 59 F2
Morotai, Pulau *Island* Indonesia 121 F3
Moscow *Capital of* Russian Federation *Rus.* Moskva 90 B4 94 B2
Mosel *River* W Europe *Fr.* Moselle 75 E5
Moselle *River* W Europe *Ger.* Mosel 67 E8 70 E4
Moshi Tanzania 55 C7
Moskva *see* Moscow
Mosquito Coast *Coastal region* Nicaragua 33 E3
Moss Norway 65 B6
Mossendjo Congo 57 B6
Mossoró Brazil 41 H2
Most Czech Republic *Ger.* Brüx 78 A4
Mostaganem Algeria 50 D1

Mostar Bosnia & Herzegovina 80 C4
Mosul *see* Al Mawşil
Motril Spain 73 E5
Moulins France 70 C4
Moulmein Burma 118 B4
Moundou Chad 56 C4
Mount Gambier Australia 130 A4
Mount Isa Australia 126 A5 130 A1
Mount Vernon Illinois, USA 20 B5
Mouscron Belgium 67 A6
Moyale Kenya 55 C5
Moyobamba Peru 40 B2
Mozambique *Country* SE Africa 59
Mozambique Channel *Sea Feature* Indian Ocean 59 F3
Mozambique Ridge *Undersea feature* Indian Ocean 49 D8
Mozyr' *see* Mazyr
Mpika Zambia 59 E2
Mtwara Tanzania 55 C8
Muang Khammouan Laos 118 D4
Muang Không Laos 119 D5
Muang Xaignabouri Laos 118 C3
Mufulira Zambia 58 D2
Mugla Turkey 96 A4
Mukacheve Ukraine 88 B2
Mulhacen *Peak* Spain 60 C5
Mulhouse France 70 E4
Mull *Island* Scotland, UK 68 B3
Muller, Pegunungan *Mountains* Indonesia 120 D4
Multãn Pakistan 114 C2
Mumbai *see* Bombay
Muna, Pulau *Island* Indonesia 121 E4
München *Eng.* Munich 75 C6
Muncie Indiana, USA 20 C4
Munich *see* München
Münster Germany 74 A4
Muonio *River* Finland/Sweden 64 D3
Muqdisho *see* Mogadishu
Mur *River* C Europe 75 D7
Murcia *Region* Spain 73 F4

Mures *River* Hungary/Romania 79 D7
Murfreesboro Tennessee, USA 28 D1
Murgab Tajikistan 103 F3
Murgab *River* Turkmenistan *var.* Murghab 102 C3
Murghab *see* Murgab
Müritz *Lake* Germany 74 D3
Murmansk Russian Federation 90 C2 94 C1
Murray *River* Australia 130 A3
Murrumbidgee *River* Australia 130 B3
Murska Sobota Slovenia 80 B2
Murzuq Libya 51 F3
Muş Turkey 97 F3
Muscat *Capital of* Oman *Ar.* Masqaţ 101 E5
Musgrave Ranges *Mountain range* Australia 129 D5
Mwanza Tanzania 55 B6
Mwene-Ditu Zaire 57 D7
Mweru, Lake *Lake* Zaire/Zambia 57 D7
Myanmar *see* Burma
Mykolayiv Ukraine *Rus.* Nikolayev 89 E4
Mysore India 116 D2
Mzuzu Malawi 59 E2

N

Naberezhnyye Chelny Russian Federation *prev.* Brezhnev 91 C5
Nacala Mozambique 59 F2
Næstved Denmark 65 D8
Naga Philippines 120 E1
Nagano Japan 110 C4
Nagasaki Japan 111 A6
Nāgercoil India 116 D3
Nagorno-Karabakh *Region* Azerbaijan 97 G2
Nagoya Japan 111 C5
Nāgpur India 114 D4
Nagqu China 106 C5
Nagykanizsa Hungary *Ger.* Grosskanizsa 79 C7
Nagyszombat *see* Trnava
Naha Japan 111 A8
Nain Canada 19 N2

Nairobi *Capital of* Kenya 55 C6

Najaf *see* An Najaf

Najrān Saudi Arabia 101 B6

Nakamura Japan 111 B6

Nakhichevan' *see* Naxçivan

Nakhodka Russian Federation 94 C3

Nakhon Ratchasima Thailand 119 C5

Nakhon Sawan Thailand 119 C5

Nakhon Si Thammarat Thailand 119 C6

Nakina Canada 18 B3

Nakskov Denmark 65 D8

Nakuru Kenya 55 C6

Nal'chik Russian Federation 91 A7 94 A4

Namangan Uzbekistan 103 E2

Nam Dinh Vietnam 118 D3

Namib Desert *Desert* Namibia 58 B3

Namibe Angola 58 B2

Namibia *Country* southern Africa 58

Nampa Idaho, USA 24 D3

Nam'po North Korea 108 E4

Nampula Mozambique 59 F2

Namur Belgium 67 C6

Nanchang China 109 C6

Nancy France 70 D3

Nānded India 114 D5 116 D1

Nanjing China 109 D5

Nanning China 109 B7

Nanortalik Greenland 62 C4

Nantes France 70 B4

Napier New Zealand 131 H2

Naples *see* Napoli

Napo *River* Ecuador/Peru 40 B2

Napoli Italy *Eng.* Naples 77 D5

Nares Plain *Undersea feature* Atlantic Ocean 15 F7

Nares Strait *Sea feature* Canada/Greenland 62 A2

Narew *River* Poland 78 E3

Narmada *River* India 114 D4

Narsaq Greenland 62 C4

Narsaq Kujalleq Greenland 62 C4

Narva Estonia 86 E2

Narva *River* Estonia/Russian Federation 86 E2

Narva Bay *Sea feature* Gulf of Finland *Est.* Narva Laht, *Rus.* Narvskiy Zaliv 86 E2

Narva Laht *see* Narva Bay

Narvik Norway 64 C3

Narvskiy Zaliv *see* Narva Bay

Naryn Kyrgyzstan 103 G2

Naryn *River* Kyrgyzstan/Uzbekistan 103 F2

Nāshik India 114 C5

Nashville Tennessee, USA 28 D1

Nâsir, Buheiret *Reservoir* Egypt 55 B2

Nasiriya *see* An Nāşirīyah

Nassau *Capital of* Bahamas 34 C1

Natal Brazil 41 H3

Natitingou Benin 53 F4

Natuna, Kepulauan *Island group* Indonesia 120 C3

Nauru *Country* Pacific Ocean 126 D3

Navapolatsk Belorussia *Rus.* Novopolotsk 87 D5

Navassa Island *External territory* USA, West Indies 34 D3

Navoi Uzbekistan *Uzb.* Nawoly 102 D2

Nawābshāh Pakistan 114 B3

Nawoly *see* Navoi

Naxçivan Azerbaijan *Rus.* Nakhichevan' 97 G3

Náxos *Island* Greece 85 D6

Nazareth *see* Nazaret

Nazca Peru 40 B4

Nazaret Israel *Eng.* Nazareth 99 A5

Nazrēt Ethiopia 55 C5

Nazwá Oman 101 E5

N'Dalatando Angola 58 B1

Ndélé Central African Republic 56 C4

N'Djamena *Capital of* Chad 56 B3

Ndola Zambia 58 D2

Nebitdag Turkmenistan 102 B2

Nebraska *State* USA 22-23 E3

Neches *River* S USA 27 H3

Neckar *River* Germany 75 B6

Necochea Argentina 45 D5

Neftezavodsk *see* Seydi

Negēlē Ethiopia 55 C5

Negev *see* HaNegev

Negro, Río *River* Argentina 45 C5

Negro, Rio *River* Brazil/Uruguay 40 D2

Negro, Rio *River* N South America 38 D3

Negros *Island* Philippines 121 E2

Neiva Colombia 38 B3

Nellore India 117 E2

Nelson New Zealand 131 G3

Neman *River* NE Europe *Bel.* Nyoman, *Lith.* Nemunas, *Ger.* Memel, *Pol.* Niemen 86 B4

Nemunas *see* Neman

Nemuro Japan 110 E2

Nepal *Country* S Asia 115

Nepalganj Nepal 115 E3

Neretva *River* Bosnia & Herzegovina 80 C4

Neris *River* Belorussia/Lithuania *Bel.* Viliya, *Pol.* Wilja 86 C4

Ness, Loch *Lake* Scotland, UK 68 C3

Netherlands *Country* W Europe *var.* Holland 66-67

Netherlands Antilles *External territory* Netherlands, West Indies *prev.* Dutch West Indies 36 C1

Netze *see* Noteć

Neubrandenburg Germany 74 D3

Neuchâtel, Lac de *Lake* Switzerland 75 A7

Neuhäusl *see* Nové Zámky

Neumünster Germany 74 B2

Neuquén Argentina 45 C5

Neusiedler See *Lake* Austria/Hungary 75 E7

Neusohl *see* Banská Bystrica

Neutra *see* Nitra

Nevada *State* USA 24-25

Nevel' Russian Federation 90 A4

Nevers France 70 C4

Nevşehir Turkey 96 D3

New Amsterdam Guyana 39 G2

Newark New Jersey, USA 21 F3

New Britain *Island* Papua New Guinea 126 C3

New Brunswick *Province*
Canada 19 F4
New Caledonia *External territory*
France, Pacific Ocean 122 C4
Newcastle Australia 130 C3
Newcastle upon Tyne England,
UK 68 D4
New Delhi *Capital of* India
114 D3
Newfoundland *Province* Canada
19 G2
Newfoundland *Island* Canada
19 H3
Newfoundland Basin *Undersea
feature* Atlantic Ocean 46 B3
New Georgia *Island* Solomon Is
126 C3
New Guinea *Island* Pacific
Ocean 126 B3
New Hampshire *State* USA
21 G2
New Haven Connecticut, USA
21 G3
New Ireland *Island* Papua New
Guinea 126 C3
New Jersey *State* USA 21 F4
Newman Australia 128 B4
New Mexico *State* USA
26-27 D2
New Orleans Louisiana, USA
28 C3
New Plymouth New Zealand
131 G2
Newport Oregon, USA 24 A3
Newport News Virginia, USA
21 F5
New Providence *Island*
Bahamas 34 C1
Newry Northern Ireland, UK
69 B5
New Siberian Islands *see*
Novosibirskiye Ostrova
New Wales *State* Australia 130
B3
New York *State* USA 21 F3
New York New York, USA
21 F3
New Zealand *Country* Pacific
Ocean 131
Neyshābūr Iran 100 D3
Ngaoundéré Cameroon 56 B4
N'Giva Angola 58 B2
N'Guigmi Niger 53 H3
Nha Trang Vietnam 119 E5
Niagara Falls *Waterfall*
Canada/USA 18 D5 21 E3

Niamey *Capital of* Niger 53 F3
Niangay, Lac *Lake* Mali 52 E3
Nicaragua *Country* Central
America 32-33
Nicaragua, Lago de *Lake*
Nicaragua 32 D3
Nice France 71 E6
Nicobar Islands *Island group*
India 117 H3
Nicosia *Capital of* Cyprus
var. Lefkosia, *Turk.* Lefkoşa
96 C5
Nicoya, Golfo de *Sea feature*
Costa Rica 32 D4
Nicoya, Península de *Peninsula*
Costa Rica 32 D4
Niemen *see* Neman
Nieuw Amsterdam Surinam
39 H2
Niğde Turkey 96 D4
Niger *Country* W Africa 53
Niger *River* W Africa
52-53 F3
Niger Delta *Wetlands* Nigeria
48 B5
Nigeria *Country* W Africa 53
Niigata Japan 110 C4
Nijmegen Netherlands
66 D4
Nikolayev *see* Mykolayiv
Nikopol' Ukraine 89 F3
Nile *River* N Africa 54 B3
Nile Delta *Wetlands* Egypt
48 D2
Nîmes France 71 C6
Ninetyeast Ridge *Undersea
feature* Indian Ocean 112 C4
117 C5
Ningbo China 109 D6
Ningxia *Autonomous region*
China 108-109 B4
Nioro Mali 52 D3
Nipigon, Lake *Lake* Canada
18 B4
Niš Yugoslavia 80 E4
Nitra Slovakia *Ger.* Neutra,
Hung. Nyitra 79 C6
Nitra *River* Slovakia
Ger. Neutra, *Hung.* Nyitra
79 C6
Niue *External territory* New
Zealand, Pacific Ocean 122 D4
127 F4
Nizāmābād India 114 D5
116 D1

Nizhnevartovsk Russian
Federation 94 D3
Nizhniy Novgorod Russian
Federation *prev.* Gor'kiy
91 C5 94 B3
Nkhotakota Malawi 59 E2
Nkongsamba Cameroon 56 B4
Nordaustlandet *Island* Svalbard
63 H2
Norfolk Virginia, USA 21 F5
Norfolk Island *External territory*
Australia, Pacific Ocean
125 E3
Nori'lsk Russian Federation
94 D3
Norman Oklahoma, USA
26 F2
Normandie *Region* France
Eng. Normandy 70 B3
Normandy *see* Normandie
Normanton Australia 126 B4
Norrköping Sweden 65 C6
Norseman Australia 129 C6
North Albanian Alps *Mountains*
Albania/Yugoslavia 81 D5
North America 14-15
North American Basin *Undersea
feature* Atlantic Ocean 46 B4
North Andaman *Island* India
117 C2
North Atlantic Ocean 62-63
North Australian Basin *Undersea
feature* Indian Ocean 124 A2
128 A2
North Bay Canada 18 D4
North Cape *Coastal feature* New
Zealand 131 F1
North Cape *Coastal feature*
Norway 64 D2
North Carolina *State* USA 29 F1
North Dakota *State* USA
22-23 D2
Northern Cook Islands *Islands*
Cook Islands 127 G4
**Northern Cyprus, Turkish
Republic of** *Disputed region*
Cyprus 96 C5
Northern Dvina *River* Russian
Federation *see* Severnaya
Dvina 61 G2
Northern Ireland *Province* UK
68-69
Northern Marianas *External
territory* USA, Pacific Ocean
122 C2

Northern Sporades *see* Voreioi
Sporades
Northern Territory *Territory*
Australia 126 A4 128 E3
North European Plain *Region*
N Europe 60-61 E3 92 B2
North Frisian Islands *Islands*
Denmark/Germany 74 B2
North Island *Island* New
Zealand 131 G2
North Korea *Country* E Asia 108
North Las Vegas Nevada, USA
25 D7
North Minch *Sea feature*
Scotland, UK 68 C2
North Platte Nebraska, USA
23 E4
North Platte *River* C USA 22 D3
North Pole *Ice feature* Arctic
Ocean 12 C4
North Sea Atlantic Ocean 68 E2
North Uist *Island* Scotland, UK
68 B3
North West Cape *Coastal feature*
Australia 128 A4
Northwest Territories *Territory*
Canada 17 F3
Norway *Country* N Europe
64-65
Norwegian Basin *Undersea
feature* Atlantic Ocean 60 C1
Norwegian Sea Arctic Ocean
13 C8
Norwich England, UK 69 E6
Noteć *River* Poland *Ger.* Netze
78 C3
Nottingham England, UK 69 D6
Nottingham Island *Island*
Hudson Strait 18 D1
Nouâdhibou Mauritania 52 B2
Nouâdhibou, Râs *Coastal feature*
Mauritania 52 B2
Nouakchott *Capital of*
Mauritania 52 B2
Nouméa *Capital of* New
Caledonia 126 D5
Nova Gorica Slovenia 80 A2
Nova Gradiška Croatia 80 B3
Nova Iguaçu Brazil 41 F5
43 F2
Nova Kakhovka Ukraine 89 F4
Novara Italy 76 A2
Nova Scotia *Province* Canada
19 G4

Novaya Zemlya *Islands* Russian
Federation 90 E2 94 D2
Nové Zámky Slovakia
Ger. Neuhäusl,
Hung. Érsekújvár 79 C6
Novgorod Russian Federation
90 B4 94 B2
Novi Sad Yugoslavia 80 D3
Novokuznetsk Russian
Federation *prev.* Stalinsk
94 D4
Novo Mesto Slovenia 80 A2
Novopolotsk *see* Navapolatsk
Novosibirsk Russian Federation
94 D4
Novosibirskiye Ostrova *Islands*
Russian Federation *Eng.* New
Siberian Islands 12 D2 93 F1
95 F2
Novo Urgench *see* Urgench
Novyy Margilan *see* Fergana
Nsanje Malawi 59 E2
Nubian Desert *Desert* Sudan
54 B3
Nuevo Laredo Mexico 31 E2
Nuku'alofa *Capital of* Tonga
127 F5
Nukus Uzbekistan 102 C1
Nullarbor Plain *Region*
Australia 129 D6
Nunivak Island *Island* Alaska,
USA 16 B2
Nuoro Italy 77 A5
Nurek Tajikistan 103 E3
Nuremberg *see* Nürnberg
Nürnberg Germany
Eng. Nuremberg 75 C6
Nuugaatsiaq Greenland 62 B3
Nuuk Greenland *var.* Godthåb
62 B4
Nyala Sudan 54 A4
Nyasa, Lake *Lake* E Africa 49 D5
Nyeboe Land *Region* Greenland
62 B2
Nyeri Kenya 55 C6
Nyíregyháza Hungary 79 E6
Nyitra *see* Nitra
Nykøbing-Falster Denmark
65 D8
Nyköping Sweden 65 C6
Nyoman *see* Neman
Nzérékoré Guinea 52 D4

O

Oakland California, USA 25 B6
Oakley Kansas, USA 23 E4
Oaxaca Mexico 31 F5
Ob' *River* Russian Federation
94 C3
Oban Scotland, UK 68 D3
Oberpahlen *see* Põltsamaa
Obihiro Japan 110 D2
Obo Central African Republic
56 D4
Oceania 124-125
Ocean Island *see* Banaba
Oceanside California, USA
25 C8
Ochamchira *see* Och'amch'ire
Och'amch'ire Georgia
Rus. Ochamchira 97 E1
Oconee *River* SE USA 29 E3
Ödenburg *see* Sopron
Odense Denmark 65 D7
Oder *River* C Europe 74 E4
78 C4
Odessa Ukraine *Rus.* Odessa
89 E4
Odessa *see* Odesa
Odessa Texas, USA 27 E3
Odienné Ivory Coast 52 D4
Oesel *see* Saaremaa
Ofanto *River* Italy 77 D5
Offenbach Germany 75 B5
Ogaden *Plateau* Ethiopia
55 D5
Ogallala Nebraska, USA 22 D4
Ogbomosho Nigeria 53 F4
Ogden Utah, USA 22 B3
Ogdensburg New York, USA
21 F2
Oger *see* Ogre
Ogre Latvia *Ger.* Oger 86 C3
Ogulin Croatia 80 A3
Ohio *State* USA 20 D4
Ohio *River* N USA 20 B5
Ohrid Macedonia 81 D6
Ohrid, Lake *Lake*
Albania/Macedonia 81 D6
Ohře *River* Czech Republic/
Germany *Ger.* Eger 79 A5
Oil City Pennsylvania, USA
21 E3
Ōita Japan 111 B6

Oka *River* Russian Federation 95 E4

Okahandja Namibia 58 C3

Okavango *River var.* Cubango southern Africa 58 C2

Okavango Delta *Wetland* Botswana 58 C3

Okayama Japan 111 B5

Okazaki Japan 111 C5

Okeechobee, Lake *Lake* Florida, USA 29 F4

Okhotsk Russian Federation 95 G3

Okhotsk, Sea of Pacific Ocean 122 C1

Okinawa *Island* Japan 111 A8

Oki-shotō *Island group* Japan 111 B5

Oklahoma *State* USA 27 F1

Oklahoma City Oklahoma, USA 27 F2

Okushiri-tō *Island* Japan 110 C2

Okāra Pakistan 114 C2

Öland *Island* Sweden 65 C7

Olavarría Argentina 44 D4

Olbia Italy 77 A5

Oldenburg Germany 74 B3

Oleksandriya Ukraine *Rus.* Aleksandriya 89 E3

Oleněk Russian Federation 95 E3

Olhão Portugal 72 C5

Olita *see* Alytus

Olmaliq *see* Almalyk

Olmütz *see* Olomouc

Olomouc Czech Republic *Ger.* Olmütz 79 C5

Olsztyn Poland *Ger.* Allenstein 78 D2

Olt *River* Romania 88 B5

Olten Switzerland 75 B7

Olympia Washington, USA 24 B2

Omaha Nebraska, USA 23 F4

Oman *Country* SW Asia 101 D6

Oman, Gulf of *Sea feature* Indian Ocean 112 B2

Omdurman Sudan 54 B4

Omsk Russian Federation 94 C4

Ondangwa Namibia 58 C3

Onega *River* Russian Federation 90 B4

Onega, Lake *see* Onezhskoye Ozero

Onezhskoye Ozero *Lake* Russian Federation *Eng.* Lake Onega 90 B3

Ongole India 117 E2

Onitsha Nigeria 53 G5

Ontario *Province* Canada 18 B3

Ontario, Lake *Lake* Canada/USA 15 F3

Oostende Belgium *Eng.* Ostend 67 A5

Oosterschelde *Inlet* Netherlands 66 B4

Opole Poland *Ger.* Oppeln 78 C4

Oporto *see* Porto

Oppeln *see* Opole

Oradea Romania 88 B3

Oran Algeria 50 D1

Orange Australia 130 C3

Orange River *River* southern Africa 58 C4

Oranjestad Netherlands Antilles 35 E5

Ord *River* Australia 128 D3

Ordu Turkey 96 D2

Ordzhonikidze *see* Vladikavkaz

Örebro Sweden 65 C6

Oregon *State* USA 24

Orël Russian Federation 89 A5

Orem Utah, USA 22 B4

Orenburg Russian Federation 91 C6 94 B4

Orense *see* Ourense

Orestiáda Greece 84 D3

Orhon *River* Mongolia 107 E2

Orinoco *River* Colombia/Venezuela 39 E3

Orissa *State* India 115 E5

Oristano Italy 77 A5

Orizaba, Pico de *see* Citlaltépetl

Orkney *Islands* Scotland, UK 68 C2

Orlando Florida, USA 29 E4

Orléans France 70 C4

Ormsö *see* Vormsi

Örnsköldsvik Sweden 65 C5

Orontes *River* SW Asia 98 B3

Orosirá Rodópis *see* Rhodope Mountains

Orsha Belorussia 87 E5

Orsk Russian Federation 91 D6 94 B4

Oruro Bolivia 40 C4

Ōsaka Japan 111 C5

Ösel *see* Saaremaa

Osh Kyrgyzstan 103 F2

Oshawa Canada 18 D5

Oshkosh Wisconsin, USA 20 B2

Osijek Croatia 80 C3

Oslo *Capital of* Norway 65 B6

Osmaniye Turkey 96 D4

Osnabrück Germany 74 B4

Osorno Chile 45 B5

Oss Netherlands 66 D4

Ossora Russian Federation 95 H2

Ostend *see* Oostende

Östersund Sweden 65 C5

Ostfriesische Inseln *Islands* Germany *Eng.* East Frisian Islands 74 A3

Ostrava Czech Republic *Ger.* Mährisch-Ostrau, *prev.* Moravská Ostrava 79 C5

Ostrołęka Poland 78 D3

Ostrowiec Świętokrzyski Poland 78 D4

Ōsumi-shotō *Island group* Japan 111 A7

Otaru Japan 110 D2

Otra *River* Norway 65 A6

Otranto Italy 77 E5

Otranto, Strait of *Sea feature* Albania/Italy 81 C6

Ottawa *Capital of* Canada 18 D4

Ottawa *River* Canada 18 D4

Ou *River* Laos 118 D3

Ouachita *River* SE USA 28 B2

Ouagadougou *Capital of* Burkina 53 E4

Ouahigouya Burkina 53 E3

Ouargla Algeria 51 E2

Oudtshoorn South Africa 58 C5

Ouémé *River* Benin 53 F4

Ouessant, Île d' *Island* France 70 A3

Ouésso Congo 57 C5

Oujda Morocco 50 D2

Oulu Finland 64 D4

Oulu *River* Finland 64 D4

Oulujärvi *Lake* Finland 64 E4

Ounas *River* Finland 64 D3

Our *River* W Europe 67 E7

Ourense Spain *Cast.* Orense 72 C2

Ourinhos Brazil 42 D2

Ourthe *River* Belgium 67 D6

Outer Hebrides *Island group* UK *var.* Western Isles 68 B2

Outer Islands *Island group* Seychelles 59 H1

Overflakkee *Island* Netherlands 66 B4

Oviedo Spain 72 D1

Owando Congo 57 C6

Oxford England, UK 69 D6

Oxnard California, USA 27 C7

Oyem Gabon 57 B5

Oyo Nigeria 53 F4

Ózd Hungary 79 D6

P

Paamiut Greenland 62 B4

Pa-an Burma 118 B4

Pachuca Mexico 31 E4

Pacific-Antarctic Ridge *Undersea feature* Pacific Ocean 123 E5

Pacific Ocean 122-123

Padang Indonesia 120 B4

Paderborn Germany 74 B4

Padova Italy *Eng.* Padua 76 C2

Padre Island *Island* Texas, USA 27 G5

Padua *see* Padova

Paducah Kentucky, USA 20 B5

Pafos *see* Paphos

Pag *Island* Croatia 80 A3

Pago Pago *Capital of* American Samoa 126 F4

Paide Estonia *Ger.* Weissenstein 86 D2

Painted Desert *Desert* SW USA 26 C1

País Vasco *see* Basque Provinces

Pakambaru Indonesia 120 B4

Pakistan *Country* S Asia 114

Pakokku Burma 118 A3

Palagruža *Island* Croatia 76 E4

Palau *Country* Pacific Ocean *var.* Belau 122

Palawan *Island* Philippines 121 E2

Paldiski Estonia *prev.* Baltiski, *Eng.* Baltic Port, *Ger.* Baltischport 86 C2

Palembang Indonesia 120 B4

Palencia Spain 72 D2

Palermo Italy 77 C6

Palikir *Capital of* Micronesia 126 C2

Palk Strait *Sea feature* India/Sri Lanka 117 E3

Palm Springs California, USA 25 D8

Palma Spain 73 G3

Palmas Brazil 41 F3

Palmerston North New Zealand 131 G3

Palmyra *see* Tudmur

Palmyra Atoll *External territory* USA, Pacific Ocean 127 G2

Palu Indonesia 120 E4

Pamir *River* Afghanistan/Tajikistan 103 F3

Pamirs *Mountains* Tajikistan 103 F3

Pampa Texas, USA 27 E2

Pampas *Region* South America 37 C6

Pamplona Spain 73 F1

Pānāji India 116 C2

Panama *Country* Central America 33

Panamá, Golfo de *Sea feature* Panama 33 F5

Panama Canal *Canal* Panama 46 A4

Panama City *Capital of* Panama 33 F5

Panama City Florida, USA 28 D3

Panay *Island* Philippines 121 E2

Pančevo Yugoslavia 80 D3

Panevėžys Lithuania 86 C4

Pangkalpinang Indonesia 120 C4

Panj *River* Afghanistan/Tajikistan *Rus.* Pyandzh 103 E3

Pantanal *Region* Brazil 36 C4

Pantelleria *Island* Italy 77 B7

Pánuco *River* Mexico 30 E4

Panzhihua China 109 A6

Papeete *Capital of* French Polynesia 127 H4

Paphos Cyprus *var.* Pafos 96 B5

Papua New Guinea *Country* Pacific Ocean 122

Paraguá *River* Bolivia/Venezuela 39 E3

Paraguay *Country* South America 42

Paraguay *River* C South America 36 C4

Parakou Benin 53 F4

Paramaribo *Capital of* Surinam 39 H2

Paraná Argentina 44 D4

Paraná *River* C South America 37 C5

Paranaíba Brazil 41 G2

Pardubice Czech Republic *Ger.* Pardubitz 79 B5

Pardubitz *see* Pardubice

Parepare Indonesia 120 E4

Paris *Capital of* France 70 C3

Paris Texas, USA 27 G4

Parkhar Tajikistan 103 E3

Parma Italy 76 B2

Pärnu Estonia *Rus.* Pyarnu, *prev.* Pernov, *Ger.* Pernau 86 D2

Páros *Island* Greece 85 C6

Parry Islands *Islands* Canada 17 F2

Pasadena California, USA 25 C7

Pasadena Texas, USA 27 G4

Passo Fundo Brazil 42 D3

Pasto Colombia 38 B4

Patagonia *Region* S South America 45 C6

Patna India 115 F3

Patos, Lagoa dos *Lagoon* Brazil 42 D4

Pátra Greece 85 B5

Pattani Thailand 119 C7

Pattaya Thailand 119 C5

Patuca *River* Honduras 32 D2

Pau France 71 B6

Pavlodar Kazakhstan 94 C4

Pavlohrad Ukraine *Rus.* Pavlograd 89 F3

Paysandú Uruguay 42 B4

Pazardzhik Bulgaria *prev.* Tatar Pazardzhik 84 C2

Pearl *River* SE USA 28 C3

Peary Land *Region* Greenland 62 D1

Peć Yugoslavia 81 D5

Pechora *River* Russian Federation 90 D3

Pecos Texas, USA 27 E3

Pecos *River* SW USA 26 D2

Pécs Hungary *Ger.* Fünfkirchen 79 C7

Pegu Burma 118 B4

Peipsi Järv *see* Peipus, Lake

Peipus, Lake *Lake* Estonia/Russian Federation *Est.* Peipsi Järv, *Rus.* Chudskoye Ozero 86 D2

Peiraías Greece *var.* Piraiévs, *Eng.* Piraeus 83 F3 85 C5

Peking *see* Beijing

Pelagie, Isola *Island* Italy 77 B8

Peloponnese *see* Pelopónnisos

Pelopónnisos *Peninsula* Greece *Eng.* Peloponnese 85 B6

Pelotas Brazil 42 C4

Pelotas *River* Brazil 42 D3

Pematangsiantar Indonesia 120 A3

Pemba *Island* Tanzania 49 E5

Pendleton Oregon, USA 24 C2

Pennines *Hills* England, UK 68 D4

Pennsylvania *State* USA 20-21

Penong Australia 129 D6

Penonomé Panama 33 F5

Pensacola Florida, USA 28 D3

Penza Russian Federation 91 B5

Penzance England, UK 69 C7

Peoria Illinois, USA 20 B4

Pereira Colombia 38 B3

Périgueux France 71 B5

Perm' Russian Federation *prev.* Molotov 91 D5 94 B3

Pernau *see* Pärnu

Pernik Bulgaria *prev.* Dimitrovo 84 B2

Pernov *see* Pärnu

Perpignan France 71 C6

Persian Gulf *Sea feature* Arabian Sea *var.* The Gulf 112 B2

Perth Australia 129 B6

Perth Scotland, UK 68 C3

Perth Basin *Undersea feature* Indian Ocean 124 A3

Peru C South America 40

Peru Basin *Undersea feature* Pacific Ocean 123 G4

Peru-Chile Trench *Undersea feature* Pacific Ocean 123 G4

Perugia Italy 76 C4

Pescara Italy 76 C4

Peshāwar Pakistan 114 C1

Petah Tiqwa Israel 99 A5

Peterborough England, UK 69 E6

Peterborough Canada 18 D5

Peter the First Island *Island* Antarctica 132 A4

Petra Jordan 99 B6

Petrich Bulgaria 84 B3

Petroaleksandrovsk *see* Turtkul'

Petrograd *see* St Petersburg

Petropavlovsk Russian Federation 94 C4

Petropavlovsk-Kamchatskiy Russian Federation 95 H3

Petrozavodsk Russian Federation 90 B3

Pevek Russian Federation 95 G1

Pforzheim Germany 75 B6

Phangan, Ko *Island* Thailand 119 C6

Philadelphia Pennsylvania, USA 21 F4

Philippines *Country* Asia 121

Philippine Sea Pacific Ocean 121 F1

Philippopolis *see* Plovdiv

Phnom Penh *Capital of* Cambodia 119 D6

Phoenix Arizona, USA 26 B2

Phoenix Islands *Island group* Kiribati 127 F3

Phôngsali Laos 118 C3

Phuket Thailand 119 B7

Phuket, Ko *Island* Thailand 119 B7

Phumĭ Sâmraông Cambodia 119 D5

Piacenza Italy 76 B2

Pianosa *Island* Italy 76 D4

Piatra-Neamţ Romania 88 C3

Piave *River* Italy 76 C2

Pielinen *Lake* Finland 64 E4

Pierre South Dakota, USA 23 E3

Piešťany Slovakia *Ger.* Pistyan, *Hung.* Pöstyén 79 C6

Pietermaritzburg South Africa 58 D4

Pihkva Järv *see* Pskov, Lake

Piła Poland *Ger.* Schneidemühl 78 C3

Pilar Paraguay 42 B3

Pilchilemu Chile 44 B4

Pilcomayo *River* C South America 42 B2 44 D2

Pillau *see* Baltiysk

Pilsen *see* Plzeň

Pinang, Pulau *Island* Malaysia 120 B3

Pinar del Río Cuba 34 A2

Píndos *Mountain range* Greece *Eng.* Pindus Mountains 61 E5 84 A4

Pindus Mountains *see* Píndos

Pine Bluff Arkansas, USA 28 B2

Pinega *River* Russian Federation 90 C3

Pineiós *River* Greece 84 B4

Pine Island Bay *Sea feature* Antarctica 132 B3

Ping, Mae Nam *River* Thailand 118 C4

Pingxiang China 109 B7

Pínnes, Ákra *Coastal feature* Greece 84 C4

Pinsk Belorussia *Pol.* Pińsk 87 B4

Piraeus *see* Peiraías

Piraiévs *see* Peiraías

Pisa Italy 76 B3

Pisco Peru 40 B4

Pishpek *see* Bishkek

Pistyan *see* Piešťany

Pitcairn Islands *External territory* UK, Pacific Ocean 123 E4

Piteå Sweden 64 D4

Piteşti Romania 88 C4

Pittsburgh Pennsylvania, USA 21 E4

Pituffik Greenland 62 A2

Piura Peru 40 A2

Pivdennyy Bug *River* Ukraine 89 E3

Plasencia Spain 72 D3

Plate *River* Argentina/Uruguay 42 B5 44 D4

Platte *River* C USA 23 E4

Plattensee *see* Balaton

Plenty, Bay of *Sea feature* New Zealand 131 H2

Pleven Bulgaria 84 C1

Płock Poland 78 D3

Prome Burma 118 A4

Prossnitz *see* Prostějov

Prostějov Czech Republic *Ger.* Prossnitz 79 C5

Provence *Region* France 71 D6

Providence Rhode Island, USA 21 G3

Providencia, Isla de *Island* Colombia 33 E3 34 B4

Provo Utah, USA 22 B4

Prudhoe Bay Alaska, USA 16 D2

Prydz Bay *Sea feature* Antarctica 133 G2

Przheval'sk *see* Karakol

Pskov Russian Federation 90 A4

Pskov, Lake *Lake* Estonia/Russian Federation *Est.* Pihkva Järv, *Rus.* Pskovskoye Ozero 86 D3

Pskovskoye Ozero *see* Pskov, Lake

Ptich' *see* Ptsich

Ptsich *River* Belorussia *Rus.* Ptich' 87 D6

Pucallpa Peru 40 B3

Puebla Mexico 31 F4

Puerto Aisén Chile 45 B6

Puerto Bahía Negra Paraguay 42 B1

Puerto Barrios Guatemala 32 C2

Puerto Busch Bolivia 40 D5

Puerto Carreño Colombia 38 D2

Puerto Cortés Honduras 32 C2

Puerto Deseado Argentina 45 C7

Puerto Maldonado Peru 40 C4

Puerto Montt Chile 45 B5

Puerto Natales Chile 45 B7

Puerto Plata Dominican Republic 35 E3

Puerto Princesa Philippines 120 E2

Puerto Rico *External territory* USA, West Indies 35 F3

Puerto Rico Trench *Undersea feature* Caribbean Sea 35 F3

Puerto Santa Cruz Argentina 45 C7

Puerto Suárez Bolivia 40 D5

Puerto Vallarta Mexico 30 D4

Puerto Williams Chile 45 C8

Pula Croatia 80 B2

Punakha Bhutan 115 G3

Punata Bolivia 40 C4

Pune India *prev.* Poona 114 C5 116 C1

Punjab *State* India 114 C2

Puno Peru 40 C4

Punta Arenas Chile *prev.* Magallanes 45 B8

Puntarenas Costa Rica 32 D4

Purmerend Netherlands 66 C3

Purus *River* Brazil/Peru 40 C3

Pusan South Korea 108 E4

Putumayo *River* NW South America 38 C4

Pyandzh *see* Panj

Pyapon Burma 118 B4

Pyarnu *see* Pärnu

Pyinmana Burma 118 B3

Pyongyang *Capital of* North Korea 108 E4

Pyramiden Svalbard 63 G2

Pyramid Lake *Lake* Nevada, USA 25 C5

Pyrenees *Mountain range* SW Europe 60 C5

Q

Qaanaaq Greenland *var.* Thule 62 A2

Qal'eh-ye Now Afghanistan 102 D4

Qamdo China 106 D5

Qandahār *see* Kandahār

Qaqortoq Greenland 62 C4

Qara Qum *see* Karakumy

Qarshi *see* Karshi

Qasigiannguit Greenland 62 B3

Qatar *Country* SW Asia 101 D5

Qattara Depression *see* Qaṭṭâra, Monkhafad el

Qaṭṭâra, Monkhafad el *Desert basin* Egypt *Eng.* Qattara Depression 48 C2 54 A1

Qena Egypt 54 B2

Qeqertarsuaq Greenland 62 B3

Qeqertarsuaq *Island* Greenland 62 B3

Qeqertarsuatsiaat Greenland 62 B4

Qilian Shan *Mountain range* China 106 D4

Qingdao China 108 D4

Qinghai Hu *Lake* China *var.* Koko Nor 106 D4

Qing-Zang Gaoyuan *Plateau* China *Eng.* Plateau of Tibet 104 C2 106 B4

Qin Ling *Mountains* China 109 B5

Qiqihar China 108 D3

Qizilqum *see* Kyzyl Kum

Qom Iran *var.* Kum 100 C3

Qondūz *River* Afghanistan 103 E4

Qondūz *see* Kunduz

Quba Azerbaijan *Rus.* Kuba 97 H2

Québec Canada 19 E4

Québec *Province* Canada 18 D3

Queen Charlotte Islands *Islands* Canada 16 D5

Queen Charlotte Sound *Sea feature* Canada 16 D5

Queen Elizabeth Islands *Islands* Canada 17 F1

Queen Maud Land *Region* Antarctica 133 E1

Queensland *State* Australia 126 B5 130 B1

Queenstown New Zealand 131 F4

Quelimane Mozambique 59 E3

Querétaro Mexico 31 E4

Quetta Pakistan 114 B2

Quezaltenango Guatemala 32 B2

Quibdó Colombia 38 B2

Quimper France 70 A3

Qui Nhon Vietnam 119 E5

Quito *Capital of* Ecuador 38 A4

Qŭqon *see* Kokand

Qyteti Stalin *see* Kuçovë

R

Raab *see* Győr

Raab *see* Rába

Rába *River* Austria/Hungary *Ger.* Raab 79 C7

Rabat *Capital of* Morocco 50 C2

Race, Cape *Coastal feature* Canada 15 G3 19 H4

Rach Gia Vietnam 119 D6

Ródos Greece *Eng.* Rhodes 85 E6

Rodosto *see* Tekirdağ

Roeselare Belgium 67 A6

Roma Australia 130 C2

Roma *see* Rome

Romania *Country* SE Europe 88

Romanovka Russian Federation 95 F4

Rome *Capital of* Italy *It.* Roma 76 C4

Rome Georgia, USA 28 D2

Rønne Denmark 65 D8

Ronne Ice Shelf *Ice feature* Antarctica 132 C2

Roosendaal Netherlands 66 C4

Rosario Argentina 44 D4

Roseau *Capital of* Dominica 35 G4

Rosenau *see* Rožňava

Rositten *see* Rēzekne

Ross Dependency *Territory* New Zealand, Antarctica 132-133

Ross Ice Shelf *Ice feature* Antarctica 132 D4

Rosso Mauritania 52 B3

Ross Sea Antarctica 132 D5

Rostak *see* Ar Rustāq

Rostock Germany 74 C2

Rostov-na-Donu Russian Federation 91 A6 94 A3

Roswell New Mexico, USA 26 D2

Rotorua New Zealand 131 G2

Rotterdam Netherlands 66 C4

Rouen France 70 C3

Rovaniemi Finland 64 D3

Rovno *see* Rivne

Rovuma *River* Mozambique/ Tanzania 55 B7 59 F2

Rožňava Slovakia *Ger.* Rosenau, *Hung.* Rozsnyó 79 D6

Rozsnyó *see* Rožňava

Rub' al Khali *Desert* SW Asia *Eng.* Great Sandy Desert, Empty Quarter 101 D6

Rudnyy Kazakhstan 94 B4

Rudolf, Lake *Lake* Ethiopia/ Kenya *var.* Lake Turkana 48 D4 55 C5

Ruiz *Peak* Colombia 36 B2

Rumbek Sudan 55 B5

Rundu Namibia 58 C3

Ruse Bulgaria 84 D1

Russian Federation *Country* Europe/Asia 90-91 94-95

Rust'avi Georgia 97 G2

Rutland Vermont, USA 21 F2

Rwanda *Country* C Africa 55

Ryazan' Russian Federation 91 B5 94 B3

Rybach'ye *see* Issyk-Kul'

Rybinskoye Vodokhranilishche *Reservoir* Russian Federation *Eng.* Rybinsk Reservoir 90 B4

Rybnik Poland 79 C5

Ryūkyū-rettō *Island group* Japan 111 A8

Rzeszów Poland 79 E5

S

Saale *River* Germany 74 C4

Saarbrücken Germany 75 A6

Saare *see* Saaremaa

Saaremaa *Island* Estonia *var.* Saare, Saarema, *Ger.* Ösel, *var.* Oesel 86 C2

Sabadell Spain 73 G2

Sabhā Libya 51 F3

Sable, Cape *Coastal feature* Canada 19 F5

Sabzevār Iran 100 D3

Sacramento California, USA 25 B6

Şa'dah Yemen 101 B6

Sado Japan 110 C4

Safi Morocco 50 B2

Saginaw Michigan, USA 20 C3

Sahara *Desert* N Africa 48 B3

Sahel *Region* W Africa 48 B3 53 F3

Saïda Lebanon *anc.* Sidon 98 B4

Saidpur Bangladesh 115 G3

Saigon *see* Hồ Chi Minh

Saimaa *Lake* Finland 65 E5

Saint-Brieuc France 70 A3

Saint Catherines Canada 18 D5

Saint-Chamond France 71 D5

St Christopher & Nevis *see* St Kitts & Nevis

St Cloud Minnesota, USA 23 F2

St-Denis *Capital of* Réunion 59 H3

Saintes France 70 B5

Saint-Étienne France 71 D5

St. George's *Capital of* Grenada 35 G5

St Helena *External territory* UK, Atlantic Ocean 47 D5

St Helens, Mount *Peak* USA 14 D3

St Helier *Capital* Jersey 69 D8

Saint-Jean, Lake *Lake* Canada 19 E4

Saint John Canada 19 F4

Saint John's Canada 19 H3

St Joseph Missouri, USA 23 F4

St Kitts & Nevis *Country* West Indies *var.* St Christopher & Nevis 35

St.-Laurent-du-Maroni French Guiana 39 H2

Saint Lawrence *River* Canada 19 E4

Saint Lawrence, Gulf of *Sea feature* Canada 19 G4

St. Lawrence Island *Island* Alaska, USA 16 B2

Saint-Lô France 71 B3

Saint-Louis Senegal 52 B3

St Louis Missouri, USA 23 G4

St Lucia *Country* West Indies 35

Saint-Malo France 70 B3

Saint-Nazaire France 70 A4

St Paul Minnesota, USA 23 F2

St Peter Port *Capital of* Guernsey 69 D8

St Petersburg Russian Federation *Rus.* Sankt-Peterburg, *prev.* Leningrad, Petrograd 90 B3 94 B2

St Petersburg Florida, USA 29 E4

St Pierre Canada 19 H4

Saint Pierre Saint Pierre & Miquelon 19 H4

Saint Pierre & Miquelon *External territory* France, Atlantic Ocean 19 H4

St Vincent, Cape *see* São Vicente, Cabo de

St Vincent & The Grenadines *Country* West Indies 35

Sajama *Peak* Bolivia 36 B4

Sakākah Saudi Arabia 100 B4

Sakakawea, Lake *Lake* North Dakota, USA 22 D2

Sakarya *see* Adapazarı
Sakhalin *Island* Russian Federation 95 H4
Salado *River* Argentina 44 C3
Şalālah Oman 101 D6
Salamanca Spain 72 D2
Sala y Gómez *Island* Chile, Pacific Ocean 123 F4
Saldus Latvia *Ger.* Frauenburg 86 B3
Sale Australia 130 B4
Salekhard Russian Federation 94 D3
Salem India 116 D2
Salem Oregon, USA 24 B3
Salerno Italy 77 D5
Salerno, Golfo di *Sea feature* Italy 77 D5
Salihorsk Belorussia *Rus.* Soligorsk 87 C6
Salima Malawi 59 E2
Salina *Island* Italy 77 D6
Salina Utah, USA 22 B4
Salinas California, USA 25 B6
Salinas Grandes *Lowpoint* Argentina 44 C3
Salisbury England, UK 69 D7
Salisbury Island Canada 18 D1
Salonica *see* Thessaloníki
Salso *River* Italy 77 C7
Salt *see* As Salṭ
Salta Argentina 44 C2
Saltillo Mexico 31 E2
Salt Lake City Utah, USA 22 B4
Salto Uruguay 42 B4
Salton Sea *Lake* California, USA 25 D8
Salvador Brazil 41 H4
Salween *River* SE Asia 104 C3
Salzburg Austria 75 D7
Salzgitter Germany 74 C4
Samaná Dominican Republic 35 E3
Samar *Island* Philippines 121 F2
Samara Russian Federation 91 C6 94 B3
Samarinda Indonesia 120 D4
Samarkand Uzbekistan 102 D2
Sambre *River* Belgium 67 B7
Samobor Croatia 80 B2
Sámos *Island* Greece 85 D5

Samothrace *see* Samothráki
Samothráki *Island* Greece *Eng.* Samothrace 84 D3
Samsun Turkey 96 D2
Samui, Ko *Island group* Thailand 119 C6
San *River* Cambodia / Vietnam 118-119
San *River* Poland 79 E5
Saña Peru 40 A3
Sana *Capital of* Yemen *var.* Şan'ā' 101 B7
San Ambrosio, Isla *Island* Chile 44 A3
San Andrés, Isla de *Island* Colombia 33 E3 34 B5
San Angelo Texas, USA 27 F3
San Antonio Chile 44 B4
San Antonio Texas, USA 27 F4
San Antonio *River* S USA 27 G4
San Antonio Oeste Argentina 45 C5
Sanāw Yemen 101 C6
San Bernardino California, USA 25 C7
San Carlos Uruguay 42 C5
San Carlos de Bariloche Argentina 45 B5
San Clemente Island *Island* W USA 25 C8
San Cristóbal Venezuela 38 C2
San Diego California, USA 25 C8
San Félix, Isla *Island* Chile 44 A2
San Fernando Chile 44 B4
San Fernando Trinidad & Tobago 35 G5
San Fernando Venezuela 38 D2
San Francisco California, USA 25 B6
San Ignacio Belize 32 C1
San Ignacio Paraguay 42 B3
San Joaquin *River* W USA 25 B6
San Jorge, Golfo *Sea feature* Argentina 37 C6
San José *Capital of* Costa Rica 32 D4
San Jose California, USA 25 B6
San José del Guaviare Colombia 38 C3
San Juan Argentina 44 B3
San Juan *River* Costa Rica / Nicaragua 32 D4

San Juan *Capital of* Puerto Rico 35 F3
San Juan de los Morros Venezuela 38 D1
Sankt Gallen Switzerland 75 B7
Sankt Martin *see* Martin
Sankt-Peterburg *see* St Petersburg
Sankt Pölten Austria 75 E6
Şanlıurfa Turkey *prev.* Urfa 96 E4
San Lorenzo Honduras 32 C3
San Luis Potosí Mexico 31 E3
San Marino *Country* S Europe 76 C3
San Matías, Golfo *Sea feature* Argentina 37 C6
San Miguel El Salvador 32 C3
San Miguel de Tucumán Argentina 44 C3
San Nicolas Island *Island* W USA 25 C8
San Pedro Sula Honduras 32 C2
San Remo Italy 76 A3
San Salvador *Capital of* El Salvador 32 C3
San Salvador de Jujuy Argentina 44 C2
San Sebastián Spain *Bas.* Donostia 73 E1
Santa Ana El Salvador 32 B2
Santa Ana California, USA 25 C8
Santa Barbara California, USA 25 B7
Santa Catalina Island *Island* W USA 25 C8
Santa Clara Cuba 34 B2
Santa Cruz Bolivia 40 D4
Santa Cruz California, USA 25 B6
Santa Cruz Islands *Island group* Solomon Islands 126 D3
Santa Fe Argentina 44 D3
Santa Fe New Mexico, USA 26 D2
Santa Maria Brazil 42 C4
Santa Marta Colombia 38 C1
Santander Spain 73 E1
Santanilla, Islas *Islands* Honduras 33 E1
Santarém Brazil 41 E2
Santarém Portugal 72 C3

Taymyr, Ozero *Lake* Russian
 Federation 95 E2
Taymyr, Poluostrov *Peninsula*
 Russian Federation *Eng.*
 Taymyr Peninsula 93 E1 95 E2
Taymyr Peninsula *see* Taymyr,
 Poluostrov
Tbilisi *Capital of* Georgia
 Geor. T'bilisi, *prev.* Tiflis 97 F2
Tedzhen Turkmenistan
 Turkm. Tejen 102 C3
Tegucigalpa *Capital of* Honduras
 32 C2
Teheran *see* Tehrān
Tehrān *Capital of* Iran
 prev. Teheran 100 C3
Tehuantepec, Golfo de *Sea
 feature* Mexico 31 G5
Tejen *see* Tedzhen
Tejo *see* Tagus
Tekirdağ Turkey *It.* Rodosto
 96 A2
Tel Aviv-Yafo Israel 99 A5
Teles Piras *River* Brazil 41 E3
Tell Atlas *Plateau* Africa 82 C3
Tel'man *see* Tel'mansk
Tel'mansk Turkmenistan
 Turkm. Tel'man 102 C2
Telschen *see* Telšiai
Telšiai Lithuania *Ger.* Telschen
 86 B3
Temuco Chile 45 B5
Tenerife *Island* Spain 50 A3
Tennant Creek Australia 126 A5
 128 E3
Tennessee *State* USA 28 D1
Tennessee *River* SE USA 29 C1
Tepelenë Albania 81 D6
Tepic Mexico 30 D4
Teplice Czech Republic *Ger.*
 Teplitz, *prev.* Teplice-Šanov,
 Ger. Teplitz-Schönau 78 A4
Teplice-Šanov *see* Teplice
Teplitz *see* Teplice
Teplitz-Schönau *see* Teplice
Teraina *Island* Kiribati 127 G2
Teresina Brazil 41 G2
Termez Uzbekistan 103 E3
Terneuzen Netherlands 67 B5
Terni Italy 76 C4
Ternopil' Ukraine
 Rus. Ternopol' 88 C2
Terrassa Spain 73 G2

Terschelling *Island* Netherlands
 66 C1
Teruel Spain 73 F3
Teseney Eritrea 54 C4
Tete Mozambique 59 E2
Tétouan Morocco 50 C1
Tetovo Macedonia 81 D5
Tetschen *see* Děčín
Tevere *River* Italy 76 C4
Texas *State* USA 26-27
Texas City Texas, USA 27 G4
Texel *Island* Netherlands 66 C2
Thailand *Country* SE Asia
 118-119
Thailand, Gulf of *Sea feature*
 South China Sea 119 C6
Thames *River* England, UK
 69 D6
Thāne India 115 C5 116 C1
Thar Desert *Desert*
 India/Pakistan 114 C3
Thásos *Island* Greece 84 C3
Thaton Burma 118 B4
Theiss *see* Tisza
Thermaic Gulf *see* Thermaïkós
 Kólpos
Thermaïkós Kólpos *Sea feature*
 Greece *Eng.* Thermaic Gulf
 84 B4
Thessaloníki Greece
 var. Salonica 84 B3
Thiès Senegal 52 B3
Thiladunmathi Atoll *Island*
 Maldives 116 C2
Thimphu *Capital of* Bhutan
 115 G3
Thionville France 70 D3
Thíra *Island* Greece 85 D6
Thompson Canada 17 G4
Thon Buri Thailand 119 C5
Thorn *see* Toruń
Thorshavn *see* Tórshavn
Thracian Sea Greece
 Gk. Thrakikó Pélagos 84 D3
Thrakikó Pélagos *see* Thracian
 Sea
Thule *see* Qaanaaq
Thun Switzerland 75 A7
Thunder Bay Canada 16 B4
Thüringer Wald *Forested moun-
 tains* Germany 75 C5
Thurso Scotland, UK 68 C2
Tianjin China *var.* Tientsin
 108 D4

Tiaret Algeria 50 D1
Tiberias, Lake *Lake* Israel
 var. Sea of Galilee, *Heb.* Yam
 Kinneret, *Ar.* Bahrat Tabariya
 99 B5
Tibesti *Mountains* Chad/Libya
 48 C3
Tibet *Autonomous region* China
 Chin. Xizang 106 C5
Tibet, Plateau of *see* Qing-Zang
 Gaoyuan
Tienen Belgium 67 C6
Tien Shan *Mountain range*
 C Asia 102 D4
Tientsin *see* Tianjin
Tierra del Fuego *Island*
 Argentina/Chile 45 C8
Tiflis *see* Tbilisi
Tighina Moldavia *prev.* Bendery
 88 D4
Tigris *River* SW Asia 92 B4
Tijuana Mexico 30 A1
Tiksi Russian Federation 95 F2
Tilburg Netherlands 66 C4
Tillabéri Niger 53 F3
Tilsit *see* Sovetsk
Timaru New Zealand 131 F4
Timişoara Romania 88 A4
Timmins Canada 18 C4
Timor *Island* Indonesia 121 F5
Timor Sea Indian Ocean
 112 F4
Timor Trough *Undersea feature*
 Indian Ocean 128 C1
Tindouf Algeria 50 B3
Tínos *Island* Greece 85 D5
Tirana *Capital of* Albania 81 D6
Tiraspol Moldavia 88 A4
Tîrgovişte *see* Târgovişte
Tîrgu Mureş *see* Târgu Mureş
Tirol *Region* Austria *var.* Tyrol
 75 C7
Tirso *River* Italy 77 A5
Tiruchchirāppalli India 116 D3
Tisa *see* Tisza
Tisza *River* E Europe *Ger.*
 Theiss, *Cz./Rom./SCr.* Tisa
 79 D6
Titicaca, Lake *Lake* Bolivia/Peru
 40 C4
Titov Veles Macedonia 81 E5
Tlemcen Algeria 50 D2
Toamasina Madagascar 59 G3

Toba, Danau *Lake* Indonesia 120 A3

Toba Kākar Range *Mountains* Pakistan 114 B2

Tobruk *see* Ţubruq

Tocantins *River* Brazil 41 E3

Tocopilla Chile 44 B2

Togo *Country* W Africa 53 F4

Tokat Turkey 96 D3

Tokelau *External territory* New Zealand, Pacific Ocean 122 D3

Tokmak Kyrgyzstan 103 F2

Tokuno-shima *Island* Japan 111 A8

Tokushima Japan 111 B5

Tokyo *Capital of* Japan 111 D5

Toledo Spain 73 E3

Toledo Ohio, USA 20 D3

Toledo Bend Reservoir *Reservoir* S USA 27 H3

Toliara Madagascar 59 F3

Tol'yatti *prev.* Stavropol' Russian Federation 91 C5

Tomakomai Japan 110 D2

Tombouctou Mali 53 E3

Tombua Angola 58 B2

Tomini, Teluk *Sea feature* Indonesia 121 E4

Tomsk Russian Federation 94 D4

Tomur Feng *see* Pobedy

Tonga *Country* Pacific Ocean 122

Tongking, Gulf of *Sea feature* South China Sea *var.* Gulf of Tonkin 109 B7 118 E3

Tongliao China 107 G2

Tongtian He *River* China 106 C4

Tonkin, Gulf of *see* Tongking, Gulf of

Tônlé Sap *Lake* Cambodia 119 D5

Tonopah Nevada, USA 25 C6

Toowoomba Australia 130 C2

Topeka Kansas, USA 23 F4

Torino Italy *Eng.* Turin 76 A2

Tori-shima *Island* Japan 111 D6

Torkestān, Band-e *Mountain range* Afghanistan 102 D4

Torneälv *River* Sweden 64 D3

Tornio Finland 64 D4

Tornio *River* Finland/Sweden 64 D3

Toronto Canada 18 D5

Toros Dağları *Mountain range* Turkey *Eng.* Taurus Mountains 96 C4

Torrens, Lake *Lake* Australia 130 A2

Torreón Mexico 30 D2

Torres Strait *Sea feature* Arafura Sea/Coral Sea 126 B4

Torrington Wyoming, USA 22 D3

Tórshavn *Capital of* Faeroe Islands *Dan.* Thorshavn 63 F4

Tortoise Islands *see* Galapagos Islands

Tortosa Spain 73 F3

Toruń Poland *Ger.* Thorn 78 C3

Toscana *Region* Italy *Eng.* Tuscany 76 B3

Toscano, Archipelago *Island group* Italy 76 B4

Toshkent *see* Tashkent

Tottori Japan 111 B5

Toubkal *Peak* Morocco 48 A2

Touggourt Algeria 51 E2

Toulon France 71 D6

Toulouse France 71 B6

Toungoo Burma 118 B4

Tournai Belgium 67 B6

Tours France 70 B4

Townsville Australia 126 B5

Towuti, Danau *Lake* Indonesia 121 E4

Toyama Japan 110 C4

Tozeur Tunisia 51 E2

Trâblous *see* Tripoli, Lebanon

Trabzon Turkey *Eng.* Trebizond 97 E2

Tralee Ireland 69 A6

Trang Thailand 119 C7

Transantarctic Mountains *Mountain range* Antarctica 132 D3

Transylvania *Region* Romania 88 B3

Transylvanian Alps *see* Carpaţii Meridionali

Trapani Italy 77 C6

Traun Austria 75 D6

Traunsee *Lake* Austria 75 D7

Traverse City Michigan, USA 20 C2

Travis, Lake *Lake* Texas, USA 27 F3

Trebinje Bosnia & Herzegovina 81 C5

Trebizond *see* Trabzon

Trelew Argentina 45 C6

Tremiti, Isole *Island group* Italy 76 D4

Trenčín Slovakia *Ger.* Trentschin *Hung.* Trencsén 79 C6

Trencsén *see* Trenčín

Trento Italy *Ger.* Trient 76 C2

Trenton New Jersey, USA 21 F4

Trentschin *see* Trenčín

Tres Arroyos Argentina 45 D5

Treviso Italy 76 C2

Trient *see* Trento

Trier Germany 75 A5

Trieste Italy 76 D2

Tríkala Greece 84 B4

Trincomalee Sri Lanka 117 E3

Trindade *External territory* Brazil, Atlantic Ocean 47 C6

Trinidad Bolivia 40 C3

Trinidad Uruguay 42 B5

Trinidad *Island* Trinidad & Tobago 36 C1

Trinidad & Tobago *Country* West Indies 35 H5

Trípoli Greece 85 B6

Tripoli Lebanon *var.* Trâblous, Ţarābulus 98 B3

Tripoli *Capital of* Libya *Ar.* Ţarābulus al-Gharb 51 F2

Tristan da Cunha *External territory* UK, Atlantic Ocean 47 D6

Trivandrum India 116 D3

Trnava Slovakia *Ger.* Tyrnau, *Hung.* Nagyszombat 79 C6

Trois-Rivières Canada 19 E4

Trollhättan Sweden 65 B6

Tromsø Norway 64 C2

Trondheim Norway 64 B4

Trondheimsfjorden *Inlet* Norway 64 A4

Troyes France 70 D4

Trujillo Honduras 32 D2

Trujillo Peru 40 A3

Tsarigrad *see* İstanbul

Tschenstochau *see* Częstochowa

Tselinograd *see* Akmola

Tsetserleg Mongolia 106 D2

Victoria Island *Island* Canada
17 F2

Victoria Land *Region* Antarctica
133 E5

Victoria Nyanza *see* Victoria,
Lake

Vidin Bulgaria 84 B1

Viedma Argentina 45 C5

Viekšniai Lithuania 86 B3

Vienna *Capital of* Austria
Ger. Wien 75 E6

Vientiane *Capital of* Laos 118 C4

Vietnam *Country* SE Asia
118-119

Vigo Spain 72 C2

Vijayawāda India 117 E1

Vila Nova de Gaia Portugal
72 C2

Vila Real Portugal 72 C2

Viliya *see* Neris

Viljandi Estonia *Ger.* Fellin
86 D2

Villach Austria 75 D7

Villahermosa Mexico 31 G4

Villarrica *Peak* Chile 37 B6

Villavicencio Colombia 38 C3

Vilna *see* Vilnius

Vilnius *Capital of* Lithuania
Pol. Wilno, *Ger.* Wilna,
Rus. Vilna 87 C5

Viña del Mar Chile 44 B4

Vinh Vietnam 118 D4

Vinnitsa *see* Vinnytsya

Vinnytsya Ukraine *Rus.* Vinnitsa
88 D2

Vinson Massif *Peak* Antarctica
132 B3

Virgin Islands *External territory*
USA, West Indies 35 F3

Virginia Minnesota, USA 23 F2

Virginia *State* USA 20-21

Virovitica Croatia 80 B2

Virtsu Estonia *Ger.* Werder
86 C2

Visākhapatnam India 115 E5
117 E1

Visalia California, USA 25 C7

Visby Sweden 65 C7

Viscount Melville Sound *Sea
feature* Arctic Ocean 17 F2

Viseu Portugal 72 C3

Vistula *see* Wisła

Vitebsk *see* Vitsyebsk

Viterbo Italy 76 C4

Viti Levu *Island* Fiji 125 F2
127 E4

Vitória Brazil 41 G5 43 G1

Vitoria Spain 73 E1

Vitória da Conquista Brazil
41 G4

Vitória Seamount *Undersea
feature* Atlantic Ocean 43 G3

Vitsyebsk Belorussia
Rus. Vitebsk 86 E5

Vladikavkaz Russian Federation
prev. Ordzhonikidze,
Dzaudzhikau 91 A7

Vladimir Russian Federation
91 B5

Vladimirovka *see* Yuzhno-
Sakhalinsk

Vladivostok Russian Federation
95 G5

Vlieland *Island* Netherlands
66 C1

Vlissingen Netherlands
Eng. Flushing 67 B5

Vlorë Albania 81 D6

Vojvodina *Region* Yugoslavia
80 D3

Volga *River* Russian Federation
94 A3

Volga Delta *Wetland* Russian
Federation 61 G4

Volgograd Russian Federation
prev. Stalingrad 91 B6 94 A3

Volkovysk *see* Vawkavysk

Vologda Russian Federation
90 B4 94 B2

Vólos Greece 84 B4

Volta, Lake *Lake* Ghana
53 E4

Volta Redonda Brazil 43 E2

Voreioi Sporades *Island group*
Greece *Eng.* Northern
Sporades 84 C4

Vorkuta Russian Federation
90 E3 94 C2

Vormsi *Island* Estonia *Ger.*
Worms, *Swed.* Ormsö 86 C2

Voronezh Russian Federation
91 B5

Võrtsjärv *Lake* Estonia 86 D3

Võru Estonia *Ger.* Werro 86 D3

Vosges *Mountain range* France
70 E4

Vostochno-Sibirskoye More
Arctic Ocean *Eng.* East
Siberian Sea 12 D2 95 G1

Vostok Island *Island* Kiribati
127 H3

Vrangel'ya, Ostrov *Island*
Russian Federation *Eng.*
Wrangel Island 12 C1 95 G1

Vratsa Bulgaria 84 C2

Vršac Yugoslavia 80 D3

Vukovar Croatia 80 C3

Vulcano *Island* Italy 77 D6

Vyatka *River* Russian Federation
91 C5

W

Wa Ghana 53 E4

Waag *see* Váh

Waal *River* Netherlands 66 D4

Wabash *River* C USA 20 B4

Waco Texas, USA 27 G3

Waddeneilanden *Island group*
Netherlands *Eng.* West Frisian
Islands 66 C1

Waddenzee *Sea feature*
Netherlands 66 D1

Wadi Halfa Sudan 54 B3

Wad Medani Sudan 54 B4

Wagga Wagga Australia 130 B3

Wagin Australia 129 B6

Waigeo, Pulau *Island* Indonesia
121 G4

Wakayama Japan 111 C5

Wakkanai Japan 110 D1

Wałbrzych Poland
Ger. Waldenburg 78 B4

Waldenburg *see* Wałbrzych

Wales *National region* UK
Wel. Cymru 69

Walk *see* Valga

Walla Walla Washington, USA
24 C2

Wallis & Futuna *External
territory* France, Pacific Ocean
122 D3

Walvis Bay Namibia 58 B3

Walvis Ridge *Undersea feature*
Atlantic Ocean 47 D6

Wandel Sea Arctic Ocean 63 E1

Wanganui New Zealand 131 G3

Wanlaweyn Somalia 55 B6